Grace
Revisited

Grace Revisited

Epiphanies from a Trappist Monk

James Behrens, OCSO

PUBLICATIONS

GRACE REVISITED
Epiphanies from a Trappist Monk
by James Stephen Behrens, OCSO

Edited by Andrew Yankech
Cover design by Tom A. Wright
Front cover photo by Katie McCarthy
Back cover photo by James Stephen Behrens, OCSO
Interior design and typesetting by Patricia A. Lynch

Scripture quotes are from the *New Revised Standard Version Bible*, copyright © 1989 by the Division of Christian Education of the National Council of the Churches of Christ of the U.S.A. Used with permission. All rights reserved.

Grace Is Everywhere was originally published by ACTA Publications in 1999. *Memories of Grace* was originally published by ACTA Publications in 2001. "Andy's Diner" was originally published in 1989 by the *National Catholic Reporter*.

Published by ACTA Publications, 4848 N. Clark Street, Chicago, IL 60640, 800-397-2282, www.actapublications.com.

ISBN: 978-0-87946-436-3
Printed in the United States of America by Evangel Press
Year 20 19 18 17 16 15 14 13 12 11
Printing 15 14 13 12 11 10 9 8 7 6 5 4 3 2 First

CONTENTS

INTERLUDE

PART II MEMORIES OF GRACE

PROLOGUE

Writing, remembering, holding for a while the memories of days gone by—these give me so much pleasure.

The discipline of monastic life might lead people to assume that the sense of who God is and what God is about becomes clearer as the years pass. It is true that the stillness and routine of the monastery does indeed gradually transform one's sense of the Divine. But it does not do so in terms of making it clearer, or easier to grasp, or more discussable. It makes it more unfathomable.

My experience at the Monastery of the Holy Spirit in Conyers, Georgia, over the past ten years or so has moved me to find words that point to an open-ended horizon, that bring God down to earth again and again. Human life transcends itself every day. God is always just ahead of our definitions, our attempts to calm the whirlwinds, our desire to hold the Spirit in our grasp.

I have always walked to my job here, which is mostly wrapping bonsai pottery that we sell. Not long ago, we moved the entire operation to a large house across Highway 212. It is a temporary move. Everything will be moved back to a new site nearer the monastery when the construction is completed. The house is about a mile from here, but I like the early morning walks. I take my time. I see things I would miss if I took a car. I walk along and think my thoughts, often stopping and looking about. A deer, a turkey, a squirrel might be enough to catch my eye. I better appreciate what I see simply because I am given the time to see it.

So one way for those who are "out in the world" (how I hate that phrase) to avoid the seemingly constant rush of life is to take a long walk every now and then. The world seems to appreciate it when we do. It slows down, shows itself, imprints itself on our heart. The mystery of life is in the details, billions of little things that, taken together, make up the scenery of our lives.

Is there a Big Picture? I used to know, but now I do not. What I do know is that the small scenes are attractive, captivating, and always near. I never have to walk very far to find them. If there is a larger, all-encompassing Story, it seems willing to recede as a backdrop to the little things that absorb us daily: things like walking, and praying, and working, and loving. We monks assume that if we gaze at the stars and ponder the meaning of life we are becoming "holy," but it is the cry of a child or the bark of a dog that truly brings us back to the Presence of God.

The following essays are of people and events that have taken hold of my heart on the road of life. Writing, like walking, demands a certain slow pace. So does reading. They cannot be done well in a rush. Life itself has a way of summoning us back to ordinary things—to our jobs, our responsibilities, our hobbies, our routines, and all that arrives through them. The starting point for an experience of God may begin when we close the books and leave behind the God of our heads. When we move back into the flow of life, we immerse ourselves in the very mystery we tried to capture in the book.

In the essays that follow, I like to think that the people and events are as revealing of the Divine as a fine sermon or theological tract. They tell of life and death, loss and recovery, hopes and frustrations, delight and disappointment. I have not changed any of them for this edition, though there have been changes over the years.

My mom and dad have passed on. Missy will be getting married in a few weeks. Hannah will soon be off to India and after that the Peace Corps. Meghan is now married to Eric and they are the proud parents of little Remick, named after my dad.

Anne is still with us here in our retreat house and is doing well. Karen, too, still works with me here with the bonsai.

9/11 forever removed the World Trade Center from the New York skyline, but workers still pour into the city every night.

We have our cats and dogs—different ones but just as much fun. Gerard still walks every day through the woods. Tom and Pablo have moved on to other places in life, and Bobby, who laughed in the rain, will be here in a week or so. He still laughs, rain or shine.

Edmond died a few years ago and I like to think he sees all he hoped to see in this life and more. Jimmy, who loved the details, also passed away. Mary, his wife, is doing well—I write to her often.

Francis Michael is now our Abbot. We recently elected him to a second six-year term. He has more gray hairs these days, and he still needs his sleep.

If you have not read the two books in which these stories originally appeared, you will meet these people in the following pages. Some think it is best not to look back in life, that it is wise to keep one's eyes on the future. But I am not one of them. These essays are all of the past, but they are also part of my present and my future. They tell where I have been and the people I have met who helped me become who I am and will continue to be a living part of me. As I reread the essays, nothing seems all that far away. Life is grace revisited over and over, a wondrous, mysterious gift that began in the primordial soup and continues until the Creator calls us all home.

James Stephen Behrens, OCSO
Monastery of the Holy Spirit
2625 Highway 212 SW
Conyers, Georgia 30094-4044
Christmas 2010

PART I

Grace Is Everywhere

FOREWORD

When I was a young woman reading *Seven Storey Mountain* by Thomas Merton, the world of Trappist monasteries held both fascination and fear. Fascination won the day, however, because I somehow knew that the world of silence and long hours of prayer, the world of spare diets and mystical awareness was not to be my world. I could look at the mystery of Trappist life from afar, in perfect safety. It was something like reading the martyrology—I was thrilled that such bravery existed and grateful that I would not be called to exercise it.

But with the increase of years and responsibilities, my repertoire of Cistercian literature also increased. I began to discover in monastic life some clues for ordering my own decidedly lay life—one filled with growing children, changing relationships, community service, workplace duties, and a longing to know God in some experiential way. I read that in the beginning monasteries were referred to as "households of faith." Was that not exactly what my husband and I were hoping to create for ourselves, our children, and all those whose lives intertwined with ours?

I supplemented my reading with visits to a nearby Trappist monastery. There I found men who—like myself—had all kinds of daily tasks to accomplish, a web of human relationships that required faithfulness to maintain, and the need to learn to recognize God in the progress of their ordinary days and nights.

A deepening knowledge of monastic spirituality helped my husband and me to name the priorities we had for our own particular household of faith. Solitude is one of those priorities. Because family life is intensely communal (as is monastic life), some attention to solitude is essential. Monks have their chapel or nearby woods—places to simply be with God. Laypeople, especially busy parents, may need to carve out such space. For both monk and layperson, solitude is not a luxury but a necessity in the quest for a balanced life. (Many Trappist monasteries, like the one in Conyers, have guest houses where men and women may come for a retreat and participate in the daily schedule of community prayer while they drink in the stillness and the solitude.)

Another priority my husband and I recognized as essential is stability—the virtue that grounds monks in the reality of everyday life. It does the same for families. Like the monastics, family members choose to cast their lots with imperfect others, to belong and to stick to one another in spite of all the idiosyncrasies and annoyances that abound in daily life.

When "worldly" Christians see how prayer (alone and with others), study, work, equality, authority and hospitality are adhered to in monastic settings, we can discern how we must order our own lives. One way that monks help us is through their own reflections and writings. *Grace Is Everywhere: Reflections of an Aspiring Monk* is a substantial contribution to understanding the mutuality between monastic life and ordinary households of faith. Father James Behrens, OCSO, has crafted these short essays as a kaleidoscope, allowing us to observe through them different facets of the sacred in the ordinary. His lens catches the stuff of life and holds it to the light of grace.

Household chores are an example. Many daily tasks are repetitive and monotonous, and most of us find ways to resist them. Behrens tells how he himself gained some insight into the value of boring work in "On Watering Plants" (p. 80). When assigned to water the monastery plants for four hours a day, he at first felt that he was just wasting time. That changed as he concentrated on the plants, discovering that each one required a different method of watering. He learned to distinguish between "good" bugs and "not so good" bugs. And he learned something else, something of lasting value—namely, that there are forms of work that must be done without hope of getting something back. "I now realize," he writes, "that such activity is how life itself thrives and blooms."

That particular vignette reminds me of a passage in Henri Nouwen's *Genesee Diary*, an account of the year he spent in a Trappist monastery in upstate New York. The abbot there assigned Nouwen to the job of loading rocks onto a pickup truck for several hours every afternoon. One day, Nouwen went to the abbot and said the rock loading was boring him beyond endurance. He wanted out. The abbot seemed pleased and replied that Nouwen's task was accomplishing its purpose and advised him to get "underneath" the boredom. I remember reading this passage at a time when I was folding dozens of diapers every day (this was in the pre-Pampers era.) I, too, was bored, but the abbot's words found resonance with me. I tried to become more attentive to my daily chore, and I found myself thinking about the countless men and women whose lives are measured by repetition. Suddenly, my isolation was pierced.

Like Nouwen, Behrens enables us to make connections in unlikely places. For example, Behrens' obvious love for the elderly monks at the Monastery of the Holy Spirit can help those of us who are trying to find ways to incorporate older parents, as well as elderly aunts and uncles and friends into our busy lives. Behrens shows us that practicing gentle respect seems the best way.

In his short piece "Edmund's Eyes" (p. 67), the author describes one evening at Compline, the final formal prayer time of the Trappists' day. The scene occurs in the darkened monastery church, with only an image of the Virgin Mary illumined. It is the old monk Edmund's turn to read a prayer. He finds his way to the lectern and stands there for several minutes turning the pages. Finally, he says softly and simply, "I cannot see." Then he repeats it more loudly. A younger monk, Joseph, comes to the lectern and reads the prayer, while the old monk stays silently by his side. In Behrens' telling of the tale, the younger monk becomes, for the moment, Edmund's eyes. "I am theoretically aware that we are one body here," he says. "I know the theology behind it and the long tradition of Christian sources that support the notion of oneness among many members. That night when Edmund said that he could not see, however, I experienced how he was literally given eyes by Joseph and how the rest of us were given a sense of what we can and do mean to one another."

Such simple gestures are the heart of a community— whether monastic or familial. And who of us, at whatever age, would not be grateful for them?

Grace Is Everywhere, amazing in its simplicity and transparency, is filled with like examples that can help all of us to see and hear the quiet movements of the Holy Spirit in the most commonplace of experiences.

In that it hints at poetry.

Dolores Leckey
Woodstock Theological Center
Georgetown University
Washington, D.C.

INTRODUCTION

My parents named me Jeff, which is how most people back in New Jersey know me. When I was very young, my mom took my sisters and brothers and me to New Orleans to visit relatives. We traveled by train. Dad stayed home because he had to work and could not get time off. The train was called the Southerner. I remember parts of that long train ride: the scenes that glided past the large train window, the warm and friendly face of a porter, the tall soft cushioned seats. I can still see the end cars winding far behind as I looked at them from the window whenever the train took a wide, slow curve.

During our stay in New Orleans, Mom took us to Audubon Park, which was not far from where she grew up and where her parents then lived. There was a large carousel there. I remember standing before that wonderful-looking ride. I looked with awe at everything about it: the painted wooden animals—horses and lions, zebras and bears—and the large seats that were carved into the shapes of ornate sleds, all fastened to shiny poles. They moved up and down on the poles as the carousel turned, and organ music played from a real pipe organ at its center. Row after row of colored light bulbs were strung across the roof, flashing red, blue, yellow and green with the rising and falling of the wooden animals.

Someone—perhaps Mom or an attendant at the carousel—helped me onto a large wooden horse. The horse was painted a shiny brown and there was a leather strap that was fastened around my waist. The ride began, the music started, and to my delight as so many things moved about me I, too, moved up and down on the horse, holding on to the shiny pole. The park about me slowly glided past trees and paths and the small crowd standing at the gates of the carousel. They were waiting for the next ride in the heat of that long-ago summer's day. I felt like the center of a moving and beautiful world, a world of lights and music and handsomely carved animals. What a ride it was, and perhaps is now, if that carousel is still there. I have been back to New Orleans many times since, but it has been a long time since I went to Audubon Park.

I still like rides of all sorts. As the years have passed, I have gradually discovered that there are many things to learn from rides. Physicists tell us that the universe is moving, that the cosmos itself is in motion, so—in the most grandiose terms possible—all that we know and love is riding along, coming from someplace and going somewhere. Little did I know as I rode that carousel that the stars far above me were moving as surely as were those colored lights right above my head.

It was easy to hold the reins of that wooden horse, and rise and fall and turn. It was also easy to sit and look out the window of the Southerner as it made its way through cottonfields and bayou country. But as I have grown over the years, the ride that is life has not always been as easy.

Much of my life has been a struggle to find and keep a certain balance. I suppose that the same could be said of any human life. We all want a smooth ride, a ride shared by those we love and who love us, a ride soothed by music and graced with color all around. We want to know where we are coming from and where we are going.

I am a Trappist monk and have lived in the cloistered monastery in Conyers, Georgia for just over four years. When I entered the novitiate, I took the name James in honor of my brother. I came here by train and remember noting that the founding monks who built this monastery also traveled here by train from Gethsemani, Kentucky, just over fifty years ago. Before I moved here, I was a priest of the Archdiocese of Newark for twenty years. I wrote the following vignettes while here in Conyers.

One morning, after completing the manuscript, I went for a ride. It was a ride with Damian, one of the monks, and it suddenly occurred to me that riding has been a key part of my life. Rides from heres to theres—on carousels and cars and planes and trains and boats—rides with bumps and lights and family and friends and ups and downs. There have been inner rides as well, rides of the heart, movements of hope and love, paths of joys and sorrows, journeys of regrets and gratitudes. I have wandered along ways of selfishness and ignorance and taken some dead ends that really hurt. But they have all been part of the ultimate mystery ride that is life.

I want to share with you the place where my ride has brought me—the Monastery of the Holy Spirit. If you ever come here, we can ride a bit, and I will show you what there is to see and experience, but you would have to stay a while and let your mind and heart journey a bit on your own.

Chances are you will not be able to do that. So, I offer the following words as my only way of taking you along with me and sharing with you some of the daily experiences of life here. There are no colored lights or shiny wooden horses at the monastery, though we do have some nice music and beautiful stars. And we monks, too, have our ups and downs. But it is a good ride, all things considered—kind of like a monastic carousel, spinning toward God, on which all that is truly human can be found and loved.

The following reflections are movements from one place to another, movements from one person's heart to the hearts of others, and, taken all together, the movement from this life to life eternal. It is for me a recurring and stunning realization that the journey of life is eternal, a ride through all that is human to that which is divine.

People who stay for a time in our retreat house often comment as to how still the monastery is. I well remember experiencing that when I came here and inquired about the life more than twenty years ago. I took a ride here and liked what I saw. But it was not time yet for me to seriously consider entering the cloister, so I rode back to New Jersey and served in several parish assignments. Then the time was right, or seemed to be, and here I am. Having lived here for a while now, I can better understand the treasure that is here. Those who visit often find that our way of life appeals to them because it allows them to slow down and find a deeper or different kind of meaning in their busy days. I often see a man or woman sitting in a chair down beside our lake, just gazing at the movement of the water and taking in the peace that this place affords. I find, though, that I want to tell visitors that the life here has its own bumps. In a culture that so prizes activity and motion to gauge accomplishment, living a simple day-to-day routine that is devoid of the typical marks of success takes some getting used to. We monks pray, study, work...and stay put. But, as I have found, such a simple routine can enhance and bring to the surface of one's heart those things that are the essence of life. Faith, hope and charity are what human beings really hunger for. Nothing else really matters. The monastic life is nothing but an expression of and an attempt to live what really matters.

DAMIAN'S STONE

Surrey Lane was the dead-end street on which I spent the early years of my life. It is the first place I remember as a "place."

We used to get bread delivered by a driver we called the Duggan Man, because Duggan's was the brand name of the bread. He was a happy and friendly man. He would stop in front of our house and go into the back of his truck and load up his tray with bread for several houses. He let us kids climb onto the truck and peek into its spacious rear.

Along the inner walls of the Duggan Man's truck were shelves, stacked neatly with rows of bread, cakes, cupcakes, coffee rings, doughnuts and cookies. The smell was wonderful. All of the boxes had cellophane tops, so it was easy to see what was in them. The iced tops of the cupcakes—soft, luscious-looking mounds and swirls of chocolate, vanilla and strawberry—always looked better than the ones our mothers made. (I am sure that we kept that opinion to ourselves, however.) My family usually got just a few loaves of bread, except for special occasions when the Duggan Man would take a cake off the shelf and deliver it to our house.

Every now and then, the Duggan Man would give us a ride. It wasn't a long ride, just a block or so to his next stop, and we stood right next to him and stared out the window at the concrete lane passing beneath the wheels. With a friendly "See you next time," the Duggan Man would help us off the truck and be on his way. It was always good to see him.

And there was the Milk Man, whose name we never knew

either. He delivered Borden's milk, and his truck was just like the Duggan's bread truck, except that it was a shiny silver color and a bit more beat up. The Milk Man came very early in the morning. On Saturdays, not school days, we would run out and greet him as he came up the street. I remember the inside of that truck, too, with its rows of glass-bottled milk, kept cool by big chunks of ice that were so clear we could see right through them. The Milk Man delivered milk and cream and juices. He would fill each order from a paper that his customers filled out and left in one of the empty bottles that he picked up the day before. He carried the fresh bottles in a metal basket, with little compartments of just the right size for the different types of bottles. The empties were left in metal milk boxes that each family kept outside, usually near the kitchen door. He would take the empties and replace them with the fresh bottles, each with a picture of Elsie the Cow, Borden's logo, stamped in red on the glass. I wonder what happened to all those milk boxes.

Mom usually placed an order just for milk, except maybe once a week when she would get a small pint bottle of heavy cream to make whipped cream. If one (or more) of us was sick or if there was a birthday, she would place an order for a quart or two of chocolate milk.

The Milk Man gave us rides, too, and I loved the sound of the jingling of the bottles as they shifted back and forth in their metal crates. The inside of the truck was cold and even in the summer months the Milk Man wore a jacket. He always stood while driving, as did the Duggan Man. All the kids on Surrey Lane wanted to grow up to be like the Milk Man and the Duggan Man. I think that we sensed that there was something good in what they did. They brought good things to people, and they seemed to have a great time doing it.

Even though I could never have expressed it in words back then, I think what I was learning was that to get anywhere you might need help, and the best help is freely given.

Much of this came back to me one day while sitting in the woods here at the monastery. The memories did not come all at once, but there was a singular event that was like a key that opened a door in my heart to memories that had always been there but had been long asleep.

The event was nothing extraordinary. It was the starting of the engine of a van. It belongs to Damian, one of our monks. He parks the van behind the retreat house, up the hill just a little ways from where I usually sit in the mornings. I did not think much about it the first time I heard the sputter, cough, wheeze and then engagement of the engine as it came to life with Damian's expertise. But the noise came to signal for me the start of another day, even more so than the monastery bell that rings at ten each workday morning. When Damian's van comes to life, it does so with a reel and a rock, and it brings me to life, too.

The van is filled with all sorts of fascinating things: empty aerosol cans, screwdrivers, oily rags, old jackets, a Mexican sombrero, a long red plastic horn, chains, hammers and tools of all shapes, ages and purposes. There are rolls of tape and old newspapers, boxes and boxes of a hundred sizes of nails and screws; metal pipes, pieces of glass, gas and electrical meters with the wires hanging loose. It contains scraps of metal, old shoes, an old battered lunch box and thermos, old blankets— indeed everything one might need to get through a day.

There is a magical quality to Damian's van. Its disarray has a beauty, a purpose that I intuit more than understand. I know that there is no other truck like his. And I also know that Damian is as unique as his van.

One morning I was walking on a road down by a hay field and I heard the van coming up behind me. I turned around and watched as it neared me. It swayed a bit as Damian maneuvered over the bumpy road. Damian's two dogs, Sasso and Bozo, occupied places of honor in the front of the van. Sasso's head was sticking out the open window of the side door and Bozo was standing on his hind legs looking out the front window at the oncoming world, his paws planted firmly on the dashboard amid the empty aerosol cans. Bozo and Sasso are mutts. They are good dogs and have a good life here. Damian takes good care of them, and they know it.

Damian pulled up next to me and asked me to hop in. I climbed into the van and after being generously licked and pawed by Bozo and Sasso, I found a place to lean and off we went. We did not go very far—just up toward the Abbey store, along the road that winds down toward the barns, and then down to the rear of the property back to the large garage where Damian has his shop and the dogs have their pen.

Damian and I chatted a bit about the weather and some other daily interests. He then asked me whether I liked the monastic life. I looked at him, smiled, and said yes I did. And it was at exactly that moment that memories of other rides I have taken began to focus more clearly. I gradually remembered with vividness the Milk Man and the Duggan Man. It was not an immediate flash of recognition, but more like a very warm and familiar sense that I had been on rides like this before, and there seemed to be a continuity, a good continuity that I wanted to understand.

So I sat in the woods on many mornings after that ride, and when I heard the sputter and roar of Damian's van, I thought about the rides we kids had on Surrey Lane, and many other rides I have taken. It occurred to me that we monks travel along a common track. In that alone, we mean much to each other. The Latin *monos* may mean "alone," but we are alone in a very close togetherness. We journey together in solitude.

I now carry in my pocket a smooth oval stone Damian gave to me. He saw me admiring it in his van and asked if I wanted one. I said yes, that it was beautiful. The next day there were four of them in my mail drawer. "Give two to your sisters and one to your mom," he said. He laughed, and then told me that they were worry stones.

It is typical of Damian to give four when asked for one. When I feel the stone in my pocket, I think of him, and of goodness and happiness, and of my sisters and our mom. It is for me not a worry stone but a memory stone.

I use Damian's stone as a stepping stone to God—as a reminder that God remembers me, even though I often forget God. I finger the stone and find it holds many warm memories. And then I say a prayer to God, who remembers always and forever.

There is a gospel account of Jesus telling the disciples about the goodness of God. If a son asks his father for bread, Jesus says, the father will not give him a stone. If a man is that good, the story implies, then how much greater is the goodness of God.

Perhaps I have been blessed with a good variation on that tale. I asked for a stone and was given just that. But the days of bread and milk and carefree rides now live in that stone in my pocket.

MISSY'S RIDE

The place was called Bond's, and it was famous for miles around for its ice cream, hamburgers and big thick malts called Awful Awfuls. It was on Valley Road in Montclair, New Jersey, where a bank now stands. That is the town where I grew up. Bond's was once listed in *Esquire*, I think, as one of the top-ten hangout spots for teens in the country. I will never fathom why it was torn down. Business was always good. I thought the place would last forever.

In the early Sixties, I must have spent the sum total of a year leaning against a bumper in the parking lot of Bond's or driving around the building, which was possible since there was only one-way traffic allowed in the parking lot. Once they exited the parking lot, most kids made an immediate right turn back onto Valley Road and drove right back into the parking lot. It was called "cruising around."

I can still hear Dad as I asked him for the family car keys on Friday and Saturday nights.

"Well, Jeff," he would say, "Where are you going tonight?"

"Just driving around," I would reply.

"Driving around? What do you mean, driving around?"

I laundered my reply a bit. I would tell him that friends and I were just going to Bond's. But we did literally drive around many a night: around the parking lot, around the block, back to the parking lot. Around and around, again and again—like that Chuck Berry song, "Round 'n' Round."

There were summer nights when well over a hundred kids

hung out in that parking lot. The smell of English Leather and Canoe, popular colognes in those days, hung heavily in the air. The cars were polished and flashy. Chinos were "in" for both genders, and the Beach Boy look was very much in vogue: Madras shirts, no shoes, full heads of hair. The Beatles and Stones were just starting to make it big, and it would not be long before our own hair grew longer and the music shifted from bebop to Liverpool. Bob Dylan's "Like a Rolling Stone" blared from the juke box, which also carried a hefty number of selections from Dion and the Belmonts, the Four Seasons, and other "safe" groups that would soon struggle to find a place on the music charts as rock music was being revolutionized.

My brother Jimmy and I took turns driving our white Chevrolet Impala—its soft green dashboard lights casting an iridescent glow and the windshield reflecting the streetlights outside. Our friends Greg and Walter sat in the back. I cannot help but think that our chats were pretty sophisticated for high-school kids. Or maybe our dads were right; maybe we just *thought* we were smart. I wonder, as we go through life do we always think we possess some sort of cutting-edge insight into the way things really are?

Once we arrived at Bond's, we would stay for hours, just hanging out and doing nothing. We had no big worries. There was a lot of music blaring from the cars. Pretty girls that we boys dreamed about were everywhere. Those July and August nights seemed like the longest and most carefree times I have ever known. Life could not have been kinder. Joe Walsh, of the musical group the Eagles, used to hang out at Bond's. I even played several times with him in a high-school band called the

Nomads, which is my only claim to near fame.

That was more than thirty years ago, as were those long, carefree rides on summer nights. Or so I thought.

A few days ago, a little girl named Missy came with her grandmother Anne to help wrap bonsai pots for us here at the monastery, which is one of our industries here, along with a bakery, a stained-glass shop, and a religious goods and bookstore.

Missy took a liking to a golf cart that we use to move pots from one location to another and begged and begged for a ride. I could not turn her down, so she hopped in next to me and we took a ride around the monastery property. She gushingly told me she was nine and could not wait to drive, to be a grownup. She showed me her multicolored fingernails. On each nail was a different design. She stretched her fingers and wiggled them. I smiled at the rapid movement of the tiny stars, rainbows, daisies and teardrops. I told her that I really understood what she meant about not wanting to wait to grow up, because there was a place called Bond's that I used to go to when I was just a bit older than she was. She asked me what I did there. I told her not much—just looked at pretty girls and tried to act cool.

She nodded her head and giggled knowingly. She asked me whether Bond's was around here. I told her no, not really, but that those kind of places find you when you need them. They are like rides in a golf cart. She looked at me, and then at her nails, thought for a moment, and said, "Uh-huh." Which I think meant yes.

Later that night I went for a long walk with Brother Mark, one of our monks. I thought of Missy, of growing up, of rides and walks and carts and bumpers, and of how many reincarnations of Bond's have come my way.

HANNAH AT THE TRAIN STATION

On my way to enter the monastery, I hitched a ride from New Jersey and stayed with my sister Meg and her family in Herndon, Virginia. She and my brother-in-law Jim have three children: Emily, Hannah and Chris. Hannah is the youngest. She was then about five years old.

I stayed in my nephew's room. Chris, then nine, amazed me with his tidiness. Everything was in order. On the ceiling in his bedroom were dozens of phosphorescent stars of different shapes that glowed in the night. The ceiling was like a planetarium. I lay awake and gazed at the cosmos above me, eventually lulled to sleep by radiant images.

Hannah sat with me in the mornings as we had breakfast. Her questions were many and amusing. She asked them in a singsong way. What is a monk? What is a monastery? Is it far? Can we visit? Do they have kids? Is there a school? Are there animals? What is a Trappist? Does that mean they are trapped?

I thought about that last one for a while.

Hannah is a very friendly and intense little girl, and I sensed that many things were churning in her mind and would eventually emerge. Her little legs swung back and forth a mile a minute as she asked one question after another. She digested what I told her along with her Wheaties and seemed satisfied as she left for school.

On the morning that I departed for Conyers, I took Meg and Jim and the kids to lunch at Union Square Station, not far from the White House in D.C. It was beautifully renovated several years ago, and there are many nice restaurants and shops. It is fun to sit and watch all the people coming and going. The ceilings are high and all the sounds of a train terminal echo throughout, adding a nice backdrop to the smaller intimate conversations taking place at the bars and tables.

Hannah fussed over her menu and eventually trusted Meg's choice for her: a hamburger and a Coke.

I knew that it would be a long time before I would be back in Herndon again. A sense of a change in our lives and ties as a family was in the air. My departing by train for Georgia was bringing all of us no small amount of heartache. It was painful because we did not know when we would next see one another.

I cannot remember what we talked about at lunch. Most surely it was small talk, carefully crafted to keep at a distance the sadness that was as real as the food before us.

Hannah pulled from her little purse a gift. It was a drawing of a lamb, done in crayons, with blue eyes and fuzzy brown fur (and, I think, shoes). She passed it to me proudly across the table and smiled. It was Lent, and I had seen the Lenten artwork from their religious-education classes taped to the refrigerator door in their kitchen. I think that she knew or remembered something about Jesus being called the Lamb of God and that impressed her. I still have the little work of art here in my room.

It was soon time to gather my belongings and catch the train. I walked to the van parked out in front, and when it came time to say good-bye to Hannah, she threw her arms around my neck and kissed me and started to cry. I was so surprised that so much had been welling up inside her. I hugged her and kissed her and told her that I would see her soon and write to her and call her and that Atlanta was not really very far. She sniffled and, after looking at Meg for a sign of acceptance of the veracity of my words, smiled a bit and nodded her head. Her tears released the same sadness and pain in me, and I was a good while on the train before my insides settled.

The sadness of that separation has receded somewhat. Hannah was here to visit just a week ago and does not remember the paper lamb. She had a good time, though, and I will write her during the week.

I will thank her for loving me, and for being my niece, and for coming so far to see me. I will thank her for that day in the train station and will ask her whether she remembers all the people coming and going and sitting and eating and laughing and crying. And I will thank her again for hugging me and kissing me and crying.

And I will write her about the Lamb.

I will tell her the Lamb is Jesus, and he gave his life for us, and is a part of us, and we are a part of each other, and that is why we laugh and cry. It hurts to be apart and feels good to be together. I will ask her never to be afraid to feel love for everything and everyone, even if it hurts sometimes, and urge her to remember that even if who or what she loves changes or goes away it is important to still love. For not many things stay the same forever, except love.

Hannah may wonder about the why and the terrible beauty of such things. And then she will know why poets write, and songs are sung, and children are fascinated by lambs, and why I boarded a train to Georgia, with her paper lamb in my pocket and my neck still moist from her tears.

CARRIED BY THE WINDS

On Sunday mornings, I usually gather a book or two and walk down to an old barn. There are several such barns here at the monastery, from the days when the monks had a dairy industry. The barns are now used for storage. One barn I particularly like is very spacious, and the rear of it opens to a large wooded area. There is a paved section in the back where I keep a lawn chair. Right next to the chair is a cinder block on which I can place my books and papers. A large iron gate is permanently open and rests against the wall. Ivy grows freely up the sides of the barn. Tree limbs have found their way into long-broken windows. The wood is old and beautiful. Everything looks just right to me—a natural kind of decay and growth. It is peaceful there.

One Sunday, I had gathered my books and was making my way down to the barn when I noticed that the skies were darkening. It looked very threatening, as if the heavens were about to open. I was anxious to get to my favorite spot, though, so I decided to risk getting wet and started on my way. I was about halfway there when, with a crack of thunder, it started to pour. A strong wind blew in from seemingly nowhere, and I knew that a severe storm was imminent. I thought it best to seek shelter, and the nearest place was the small porch behind the monastery store. As small a place of refuge as it is, it would offer some shelter from the wind and the rain. I ran for it and had no sooner stepped under the roof when the rain came down in torrents and the wind reached gale force. Trees were swaying and entire branches started to tear away from their bases and fly through the air every which way. I could do nothing but sit and wait it out and try to keep as dry as possible. I did not mind. It was something, that storm—how quickly it had arrived and how fierce it was. I liked watching it.

I marveled at how the wind forced so many things in its path to bend, to make way for its power. I saw what I thought were bits of paper or perhaps large leaves in the distance buffeted by the wind. But as they came closer, I realized that they were birds. I watched them, fascinated by how they seemed to have mastered a way to allow the wind to carry them. Even though they were tossed around a bit, they managed to right themselves and move ahead, carried along by something far stronger than themselves. They had learned to make good use of the winds that carried them. I had the sense that even if the wind tired of them, it could not blow them from the sky. The birds knew too well how to maneuver, how to rise and fall and sway with every shift in the wind's direction and velocity. The birds passed above me, and then rode the winds on toward the main building.

Eventually the skies cleared, and I headed down to my chair in the barn, avoiding the large puddles and small rivulets of water that had formed so rapidly. By the time I got to my chair and sat down, little birds were bathing and drinking in the puddles behind the barn.

There are other winds that sometimes blow within me: winds of anxiety and worry, fear and mistrust, anger and regret. They can easily dislodge and disperse whatever peace I may think is mine.

Birds are wise. They do not flee the wind—they use it well,

ride with it, and get where they need to go. They carry no books or papers or maps to guide them—just instinct that frees them to trust the wind.

A monastery is a place to become familiar with the winds, to grow wise as to their sudden appearance, ferocity and shifts in directions. The wisdom is to be still and not run, to befriend the winds and be carried by them. Eventually they bring us to places of refreshment and cleansing.

THE MONK WHO NEEDS HIS SLEEP

One day while I was chatting with Francis Michael, one of our monks, he told me how upset he was because he found it very difficult waking up for the early hour of vigils. The monastery bell rings at 3:45 every morning, and he occasionally sleeps through both that and his alarm. He revealed this to me one afternoon, after I had shared with him some things about which I had been very anxious.

I had wanted to speak with Francis because he is blessed with a receptive heart and a generous ear. When he walks into a room, a warmth enters with him.

When I first came to the monastery, the idea that Jesus prayed in me through his Spirit helped a lot. I wanted then and want now to let him "be" in me, and to use my life, my time, my words, my very self as he may see fit for his self-expression. Yet I still sense within me a strong attachment to finding the "right" words, the "right" time, the "right" everything. So I do not feel as trusting of Jesus as I perhaps should be. I know he is within me, even before I think of him or worry about his presence. So why do I not simply trust his movement in my heart?

It is easy for me to awake every morning. I do so much earlier than I need to. It comes naturally. I would like to think that, just as Jesus may need to awaken early in me, he may choose to sleep a while longer in the heart of my fellow monk. That Jesus lives in Francis Michael is obvious.

Maybe I would be less anxious if I slept a bit more and worried less.

SINGING WITH TOM

Brother Tom has a voice of pure gold. He is our cantor. The quality of his voice is as rare as it is good. He sings with his heart. Each word that he sings seems crafted and lingers in the air for a brief but beautiful moment and then fades gracefully to make room for the next word. When strung all together, the chant is divine expression. Tom's gift endows our chanting in choir with everything a seeker of prayerful psalmody could hope for. He brings to his words genuine expressions of joy, pain, loss and hope. They come from a place in his heart where he has known them. He takes the range of human experience that can be found in the psalms and lifts them from the text with the careful and tender use of his voice. His words carry these psalms from us to God.

I used to sit across from Tom in choir and loved to watch him sing. His eyes close as he sings. His right hand makes the slightest movements in the air, as if placing the perfectly pure notes in some magical place before him, where they rest ever so briefly before taking flight after the other still resonating notes.

I do not know whether Tom ever struggled to find that voice that seems to come to him so naturally. He does more than sing well. He knows how to give certain words and phrases a hauntingly exquisite cadence that is just slightly out of syncopation with the organ, and the result is something mystical.

Now, for the past few months I have been sitting next to Tom in the choir, and he has been gradually working me into the repertoire of psalmody. I found one day that I was leaning toward him, as if his voice was drawing me to him, and a memory from long ago came back to me that was painful in its vividness.

I used to sing with my twin brother, Jimmy, who was killed in a car accident thirty years ago (on his way home from Bond's ice-cream parlor one night). We sang well together. Harmony came easily to me. I would sing the high parts, and Jimmy sang the low. Our voices were as identical as our faces, and I would always lean as close to him as possible to keep on key. Jimmy's voice was strong, and just singing with him enhanced the strength, force and direction of my own. Without my ever being aware of it, Jimmy was crafting my voice, guiding and toning it. He was making it like his own while at the same time building my confidence.

I had long forgotten what it was like to sing with him, though I have so missed the life that we had together.

When that flashback happened and I realized who it was I last leaned into while I sang, my eyes filled with tears. I do not think that anyone saw. I pulled out a handkerchief and wiped my eyes and blew my nose as if I had a slight and sudden cold. But in a strange way, my heart was elated. I had once again found someone to truly sing with, and it is still a beautiful experience.

Not too long ago, Tom shared with me that he wanted to write and that he was struggling with words and ideas and sentences and, above all, confidence. I had heard him tell me stories about his youth, stories that were human and interesting, and I told him to trust his words and his memories and just write, and then write some more, and then go back and write again, and then pass it around to some people he trusts to get feedback.

He is, in short, struggling to find a voice that does not come as readily to him as his chant voice.

I hope Tom can lean into me and write. The words are all around him, right next to that magical place in the air where he so lovingly places his notes.

Strange the things we carry about us, things that are very real and about whose presence and power we have little, if any, inkling. By loving song and being so generous with it, Tom actually improves the voices of others. He sings and others follow—and the others sing more beautifully. It is that simple.

We teach one another every day, simply by doing what we love and in so doing impart our best.

THE LIVING CROSS

During a recent trip, our Abbot, Dom Bernard, lost his pectoral cross. He spoke about it during our Sunday morning chapter when he returned and said he felt bad because of the many memories he associated with the cross. He explained the circumstances of its loss and then said with gratitude and more than a trace of fondness that he hoped whoever finds it might benefit from it as much as he had.

I wondered as the abbot spoke if the cross would ever be found and returned. But as Dom Bernard let his possession go with a wish of well-being for its finder, something else stirred within me—a blend of admiration and guilt.

The more I get to know of my fellow monks, the more I admire the grace with which they give of everything, even their losses. Whoever finds Dom Bernard's cross will also find the special blessing that comes with everything he touches.

The more I get to know myself, on the other hand, the more I realize how far I have to go in learning to cope with even the little things I lose or have lost along the way. I am not sure how I will ever cope with the loss of bigger things—time, memory, my loved ones, my life itself.

I know that taking Jesus to heart is the secret to it all. I have learned as much from observing our monks. Knowing Jesus makes all kinds of losses bearable, even though such losses may cut very deeply into the heart.

The cross is a reminder that, try as we might to keep what we are and have, eventually we stand to lose it all. It is a freeing wisdom to live in such a way that our lives are transparent enough to allow God to shine through as the single truly important possession.

Every now and then we are graced with people who not only wear a cross but have learned to take it to heart. For most of my life, the best gifts I have received have been abstract things—realities that are self-contained. Peace, goodness, charity and hope, for example, have come my way only as I have experienced them in and through the lives of others.

Listening to Dom Bernard that morning, I suddenly realized that all gifts that are of God and given through the Spirit are the very life and reality of Jesus. He is peace, he is goodness, he is hope, he is charity. These do not exist apart from him.

"God alone." Those two words are a prayer that says it all.

The cross is a living, loving and redemptive mystery. The cross is the life of Jesus in each of us. If I learn to take my crosses to heart, I am allowing Jesus his rightful home there...and I can never lose him.

PEEWEE'S LAUGH

Peewee is a layman. He and I work together at the monastery, in the old barn where we store our bonsai pots. We wrap and ship bonsai pots and other accessories to places near and far. There was a major fire in that area last November, and since then we monks have needed all the help we can get. It might be said that the wind that fanned the fire that night in November kept on blowing long after the flames were put out, but in this case the bad winds turned good. They brought Peewee.

In an article about the late Frank Sinatra, the singer was quoted as saying that he often heard music and notes in his head and was mystified as to where such beauty came from. At times I experience such music, too, but there are times these days when laughter enters my mind as well. Peewee's laugh rings in my ears and lingers warmly within me long after he has gone home, and the thought of him laughing always makes me smile.

Peewee does not have much money and has not traveled much. I do not know whether he envies those who have. He has never said. He takes a delight in the simple, everyday things of life. I like to hear him speak of such things.

His laugh makes me wonder about what it means to be human.

We suffer from a strange vision of the ideal human as being complete, self-contained, fulfilled and satisfied. Then we strive to reach that goal ourselves. This road to the attainment of self-sufficiency is, for many of us, believed to be found through wealth. Yet the goal seems to be always just ahead of us, as if on a constantly receding horizon that never comes closer or gives way to our weary feet. No matter what we accumulate or from whom we ask directions, we never find happiness.

Peewee will never walk such a road. He is well on the way to somewhere else, laughing here and there along the way.

I suppose Peewee thinks me to be a religious man and considers this monastery to be a religious place. Yes, I think about God. And, yes, this place is special to anyone who comes here. I suppose that my being a part of it involves me in something religious. The monastery is often a heady enterprise, a road of words and rituals and meetings and elevated discourse. But something in the very depths of our humanity bids us monks stop and look down at our very feet, at the road we are all on. Peewee's laughter, his lightheartedness and joy, invite us to listen to something of God that is different from the world's idea of human success.

The road to the Kingdom is toll-free. There is no "getting" it or even losing it. It is ours as we live it. We find it when we live in our incompleteness and our need for one another. It is an easy road to find. One of the signs that point the way is Peewee's laughter.

ABIDING BEAUTY

The world will be saved by beauty.
—Peguy

One afternoon, I stood in what was once a beautiful garden. I had been told that it had been the pride and joy of a man who was now an old monk. I had seen photographs of it and indeed it was truly beautiful. Every imaginable color burst forth from so many plants and flowers. Paths cut through the garden, paths now overgrown with weeds and fallen leaves, but even the paths were laid out by the monk with an obvious eye for loveliness. They twisted and turned, carefully laid out beneath the shade of the large trees, no part of them exposed to the heat of the sun.

There were several old benches on which no one rested anymore.

There are far fewer monks now than when the monk was young, and the ones that remain have little time to rest. When they do rest, it is done in other places on our grounds.

The monk's garden has long since been abandoned. I was there to tidy it up as best I could, but I did not know where to begin. I raked a bit, pulled a few weeds, and then sat on one of the benches. I heard a noise and turning around saw the old monk standing behind me, leaning on his cane and pointing out a particular tree to me. He smiled as he spoke and said that he had planted that tree years ago. His kind, blue eyes sparkled, and he seemed oblivious to the ruins that surrounded him. He whispered the name of the tree, a name I had never heard, with a kind of love. He raised his voice just a bit and continued to speak to me, telling me what plants were once where, and how he loved keeping the place beautiful. But, he said, he was now too old and had to let the garden go.

His hand must have grown tired, for he soon placed it on top of his other hand and leaned on his cane. The cane shook slightly. He smiled at me, told me to do what I could, and then shuffled off.

Our years pass quickly. We are given just so much time and strength to tend our garden. With care and patience, beauty is trimmed and managed and brought to an artistically inspired fruition. The garden then stands proud and affords passers-by a place to sit and wonder about their lives. Then, like those lives, the garden fades.

Days later, near sunset, I entered the garden again and the old monk was sitting on a bench. He saw me and smiled, and, raising his cane, pointed to the setting sun, a huge ball of red fire sinking beneath a cloudy sky. "It is so beautiful," he said, and smiled again. I sat next to him, and we spoke for a while of the things of that day. He listened, but his eyes were fixed on the sun.

I have a feeling that my brother monk is now beyond all that surrounds him. There was once a sure reciprocity that existed between his concerns and his garden. He did his bit when it was time to do so, and now seemed to relish basking in a more enduring beauty, symbolized perhaps by the setting sun that would surely rise again the next morning.

Beautiful things indeed abound. Thank God for the many

who create things of beauty and who open our eyes and hearts to all the beauty that there is. But there is another kind of beauty that is coming, that our years and cries summon, a beauty that shall seize us and enrapture us. It makes eyes sparkle and moves an old monk to whisper with love to a tree that will one day die.

PABLO'S SONG

Those who seek the solitude of the desert, who intentionally go off to a faraway place, do so because they feel drawn by the mystery of God. God whispers to them, and they leave all that is familiar. They retreat to listen and know better the One who calls, who whispers, who bids come.

The monastery is not as remote or as desolate as a desert. There are, ironically, times when it is not even easy to find a genuine place of solitude. There are always sounds—of cars in the distance, of jets passing overhead, of church bells that toll. The raising of one's head can always afford a glimpse of a monk or two in the distance, quietly walking on one of the many paths here that wind through the woods. It is necessary, then, for a monk to find for himself a place set apart, a place that is his own, where the raising of his head affords nothing but a view of the trees and where the sound of cars and jets can seem distant enough to be a part of another world.

I have found such a place, deep in the woods, an easy walk from the main monastery buildings. I go there often and sit and let peace take hold of my heart and whisper what it will. The peace is not a voice but indeed a whole new language—a language that uses the wind as a tongue, the leaves as syllables, the birds as laughter, the bees as a hum, the greens and browns of the forest as tones of passion and desire, the smells and musty vapors of the dense woods as sweet breath.

Late one evening, I was sitting and listening in the woods to the birds and other creatures speak their languages. The day was done, and I do not know why the creatures speak then, for I know that they, too, rest at night, putting aside until the coming of the morning their search for mates and food. But the late evening is always a time for singing, too. I like to think that perhaps there are some lonesome doves among the animals who are hoping to find some comfort before the sun sets and darkness descends.

Suddenly I heard the sound of a human voice, a man singing. He was not far off, though the sound easily carried throughout the woods. I assume that he thought that no one was near enough to hear him. It was Pablo, one of our monks. He was singing a hymn to Mary in Spanish in his deep, rich voice, which, on that evening, was more beautiful than ever. His words left his heart and moved through the woods as if looking for the woman he sang to that night with such tenderness and love.

For an instant, Pablo's voice blended with all the other sounds of that evening. There was no separation from the songs of the birds, the gentle rustling of the leaves, the laughter of a nearby creek. It all comprised a single evening song, a song of all that is lovely and forever and unseen. It was as if every living creature around me shared in the very heart of being, the heart of God, who gives voice to both singing monks and chirping birds.

Be alone somewhere and listen to that song.

LATE AFTERNOON LIGHT

It was late afternoon, and the rays of the setting sun shone through the stained-glass windows of the monastery church, coloring the walls and floor with beautiful pastel colors. Blues, greens, reds and yellows rested and blended with ease on the tall white concrete walls. The wooden choir stalls looked as if they had been adorned for an evening out on the town. They basked in a dazzling array of color.

I sat near the front, not far from the altar of reposition where the Eucharist is kept. I had the church to myself. The day's work was done, and it would be another half-hour before the rest of the monks came into the church for Vespers.

Gazing at the burning candle near the tabernacle, I wondered about the meaning of the true presence of the risen and glorified Christ, made so through the consecration of bread and wine.

One of our monks walked in. He caught my eye as he walked into the church from the cloister and gently smiled at me and slowly continued his way across the front of the church. The sunlight noticed him, too, and played on his habit as he walked. He stopped before the Blessed Sacrament, bowed very low, then straightened up and continued on his way to his place in choir, far behind where I was sitting that afternoon.

I could feel his presence in the church. His sitting behind me transformed the atmosphere. I felt especially close to him, and allowed his presence to touch me as deeply as I could. I prayed for him, for his well-being, for whatever hopes he harbored in his heart that day. Yet I knew that I would never tell him any of that.

The monastery is a place where, among other things, one comes to terms with oneself in solitude. One must also, however, come to terms with others. A monastic enclosure invites you to live essentially—with only the very basics of human, and therefore social, existence. There are not many things that we monks do for one another. We do not exchange gifts, for example. Ours is not a competitive life; there are no career tracks, no special hats to wear. And so there is a minimum of ulterior motives regarding human relationships. You cannot use another man to get someplace or to secure something other than simply being a friend.

In the quiet of that church that afternoon, amid the play of light on the walls, I prayed. There is a light in each of us, a light that is somehow in everything and in everyone. It attracts, warms otherwise cold and lifeless words and actions, and offers a context for beauty, truth and desire. It illumines parameters for restraint, limits and silence. It offers a way of discernment, of simply knowing that we are not the masters of our origins or ultimate destinies. The light can catch us unaware and leave us to give pause and marvel at its loveliness…and encourage a smile, a bow and a slow walk in silence.

In the fading light of a late afternoon, I saw a monk who gave his life to a God no one of us truly knows.

Who are you, Lord Jesus? Your presence and our lives are inseparable. We, too, are living tabernacles, upon whom your light shines. We cannot understand a Eucharistic presence apart from your presence everywhere.

My friend, my brother, smiled at me and bent his body before you. I smiled back and prayed.

SPIDER WEBS

Personal space, a bit of land, a home, a soft living-room chair before a fireplace, a winter's scene outside the window, a book in one's lap, all blending together to make for a near-perfect American dream. Sigh.

I confess that I have wanted such, but have only been able to get bits and pieces of it. When I entered the Monastery of the Holy Spirit, however, I had to divest myself of even those. I left the fireplace behind. The books I donated to a library. Most of the other things I gave to friends. Can't have much here in a monastery—there is simply no room for it.

I never really had a home of my own, though the thought of having one is something that still crosses my mind: a nice little fence and mailbox; neighbors who wave hello as they walk their doggies; the paper boy or girl, wearing a baseball cap and riding a red bike, shouting a friendly "Hi, Mr. Behrens!" as the *Evening Star* is tossed across my well-kept lawn; frosted windows on a wintry morn; little neighborhood kids coming by dressed as witches, ghosts and goblins on Halloween, giggling at ol' friendly Mr. B., as I would surely be known. The sound of a train whistle in the distance would be a nice touch.

I would answer the door wearing my favorite old sweater with a pipe in my mouth. My wife, June, would be at my side, smiling at the little ones. Our dog, Ruff, would bark just a bit, raising his head off the parquet floor.

Are Tommy Hilfiger sweaters still in?

Oh, well.

I sat on the retreat house porch every morning for about two weeks when I first came here. There were several rounds of interviews I had to go through before I was notified of my acceptance into the community. I had left a lot of stuff in New Jersey, and I worried about it constantly during those weeks. I eventually did go through a minor version of hell getting rid of it all, and it took me a while to feel good about it. Now it is all gone, except for a few mementos I am glad I kept.

On the porch every morning I had coffee and a few cigarettes and looked out over a beautifully kept garden. One morning I noticed the spider webs. I suppose that they were there every morning, but I did not notice them right away. There would usually be two or three stretched between the porch and some nearby trees. The webs were huge, about two to four feet across. The spiders were not all that big. But they sure could weave. They were dwarfed by their own creations. I sat transfixed at the intricate patterns of the webs—tiny rectangular shapes, hundreds of them, all connected to form a precise circle. The dew made them glisten and added an extra touch of beauty.

One morning I went out later than usual, just to look at the webs, and they were all gone. I could not imagine what had happened. Maybe they had some substance that made them dry up easily? Or had someone knocked them down? Was the wind the culprit? Or one of the monks? I was intrigued.

So, the next morning I went out earlier, and the webs spun during the night were there. All new ones. I sat down with my coffee and cigarette and waited and watched. The sun rose higher, and soon enough I had my answer.

One by one, the spiders somehow ingested their own webs.

I am not sure whether that is the right word. But I saw them put their webs into some orifice as they very patiently moved across and up and down them—an amazing sight. The webs gradually vanished.

I thought a lot about myself, watching those spiders that morning and several mornings thereafter.

There I was, worrying about the once-in-a-lifetime move I was about to make, and here were these creatures who had to go through such travail every morning of their lives. Imagine having to cram your house and all your belongings into yourself every morning? And then rebuild it every night? And rebuild it perfectly? I laughed at myself.

Pity the poor spider, who has no home to call its own.

Pity those of us who do and are stuck with it and all our stuff.

THE MAN WHO LAUGHED
WITH THE RAIN

Just at the bottom of a fairly steep path that winds down toward the lakes behind the monastery buildings is a large shed. It is used to store some old machinery. There are a few buckets and a large wooden barrel. It is a good place to read. I can sit on the barrel and read for several hours, taking in the peace around me. On a hot day, the shade cools things off a bit. On a windy day, the shed affords some shelter from the wind. And on rainy days, the shed keeps my book and me dry.

There was a young man at Mass this morning. He was in a wheelchair. He wheeled himself into the monastery church and took a spot near the sanctuary steps. He appears to be in his late twenties and severely crippled with muscular dystrophy. I recognized him from earlier visits. He waved to the monks as they processed in for Mass, and several of the monks went over to greet him. He looked up at them and smiled, raising his arms and waving, elated that he was personally welcomed. I greeted him as I later walked up the stairs to the sanctuary, and he extended his hand to me. He had difficulty grasping my hand, so I simply took his in mine and we shook. He smiled.

He went his way after Mass, back to the retreat house where he was staying. I busied myself the rest of the day, not thinking about the young man at all.

I was in the shed later that night reading a novel. I found it hard to get into the book. My mind was still racing from some scattered and insignificant events of the day. Morning Mass seemed like ages ago.

The day had been full. I had to take out the garbage, run some things off on the copier, do my laundry, and finish up some other odds and ends that I usually leave to the weekend. The book stayed open in my lap, and I gazed around me. I brushed away an occasional mosquito or a restless wasp. Some little birds flew into the shed and made straight for a pile of sand. There were three of them, and they found a spot in the sand, wiggled around as if cleaning themselves, flew away, and then returned to the same spot and did the same thing. Several deer grazed lazily not too far down the road, oblivious to my presence. The geese and ducks made their occasional racket down near the lake. I just sat there taking it all in.

Clouds were gathering. I looked up and saw diminishing patches of blue. The first drops of rain surprised me, since the skies were not all that ominous. The rain tapped the tin roof of the shed, falling lightly and evenly. Then I heard thunder, and the sky did begin to darken. Storms can arrive in Conyers in a matter of minutes. I looked at my watch and grew anxious that I would get caught in the rain and not be able to make it back on time for night prayers.

The even cadence of the drops swelled to a roar as gallons of rain pelted the tin roof of the shed.

Movement on the road caught my eye. Someone was pushing the young fellow from Mass in the wheelchair. They could not see me. Suddenly, they stopped, both drenched. The man in the wheelchair raised his arms to the heavens, his face broke into a smile, and he started to laugh. He waved his arms, as if welcoming some unseen presence that lived in the rain. This went on for a few seconds and then the two proceeded on their way back up the hill to the monastery, to the warmth and shelter of the buildings.

Seeing this man welcome the rain yanked me right out of my own little world. There I was, in my sheltered shed, worrying about getting wet, when an angel on wheels arrived, a friend to misfortune, to laugh and wave his weakened arms in ecstasy.

Long ago, I read that only Revelation can reveal Revelation. The One who reveals must speak. I have read the Book of Revelation, have said a lot of fancy things about it, and can quote chapter and verse. But I cannot say that the One who spoke was revealed to me—until tonight.

Tonight, the veil parted just a bit. I pray that I now know just a little something of the reality of God.

THE KITTEN IN THE DUMPSTER

Not long ago I had to haul a heap of garbage to a green metal dumpster that is parked behind the retreat house. Just as I was about to empty the contents of a large garbage can into the dumpster, I heard a muffled cry and then a "meow" coming from the depths of the huge bin. I looked over the edge and scanned every nook and cranny of refuse, but I could not see the kitten. I knew it was there, however, for I soon heard the shifting sounds of garbage and saw a small mound of paper and trash in the corner move.

Mike, a layman who is the retreat house cook, saw me from the window and knew that something was amiss. He came outside and asked if he could help in any way. Then Karen, a frequent guest at the monastery, came from the kitchen. Karen is in the military, and without further ado she climbed into the dumpster and foraged through the rubbish for the kitten. She found it, and it scampered from one end of the dumpster to the other. It was a cute gray kitten, only a few weeks old. I was amazed how such a little creature possessed such dexterity.

Karen leaped across the goo and lunged for the kitten and succeeded in grabbing him. Once lifted from the rubbish, the kitten began to cry and scratch and bite Karen's hands. I suppose that he thought himself to be in even more of a predicament than being trapped in a dumpster. I am quite sure that Karen's hands were his first contact with humans, a species he had carefully avoided thus far in his young life.

Mike threw a towel to Karen, and she carefully wrapped

the kitten and tried to soothe him with soft words. She held the bundle close to her body, and he soon calmed down and just stared at his captor, his eyes wide and very frightened. Karen climbed out of the dumpster and freed our little friend. He scampered off into the woods, stopping at the tree line, looking back at us for a few seconds, and then running off into the shelter of the trees. I am sure that I will see him again very soon, but am also sure that he will avoid that dumpster for the rest of his life.

How strange and frightening we humans must seem to other creatures, especially when they fear that we will harm them.

Later, I thought about God and humans. Here we are, trapped in this walled expanse of life, a place we try to dress up as much as possible. Fear of loss makes us do terrible things to ourselves and to each other. Those of us who live fairly peaceful lives know well that there are other areas that gnaw at the fringes of our composure. Our peace is relative, provisional, fragile—often lived at a terrible expense to others. We do not yet share this walled existence very well.

Grace abounds in the world. Like Karen with the kitten, God has reached into the dumpster that is the world and then climbed in and stayed. That presence has made love stronger than fear. It is a love that can and will outrun our most feverish attempts to flee.

Maybe that little kitten had a second thought looking back in that instant before he dashed to his freedom in the woods. Maybe he sensed that we humans are not so bad after all. Neither, perhaps, is God.

EDMUND'S EYES

Edmund is one of the senior monks at the Monastery of the Holy Spirit. The way he walks, smiles, listens, speaks—all emanates from a deep and gentle way that is simply Edmund.

One night it was Edmund's turn to read the closing prayer at Compline, the seventh and last prayer of the day. He moved in the darkened church to the lectern and slowly opened the book of prayers. We could hear the pages turn as he tried to find the right spot. After about two minutes, he raised his head and spoke into the darkness. "I cannot see," he said softly. And then again, louder, "I cannot see."

Immediately, another monk, Joseph, came to the rescue, and as Edmund stepped to the side the prayer was read. Edmund bowed his head and prayed with the rest of us. Afterward we left the church as we do every night, as one body in a single file, bowing before the Abbot for his blessing and then heading upstairs to bed and sleep.

I am theoretically aware that we are one body here. I know the theology behind it and the long tradition of Christian sources that support the notion of oneness among many members. That night when Edmund said that he could not see, however, I experienced how he was literally given eyes by Joseph and how the rest of us were given a sense of what we can and do mean to one another.

I have so often seen here a lived and deep sense of shared life, of a truly common body. It is as commonplace as the air we breathe. The strong members of the community give freely to the weaker ones, and the weak ones give the strong a living example of the gentleness and wisdom that comes with accepting human limitations.

Some day, I hope to see as Edmund sees.

SIGNS OF LIFE

Many months ago, my sister Mary brought a small tree that belongs to a friend of hers to our bonsai shop at the monastery. The tree was in very bad shape, withered and brown, with hardly a trace of life to it.

One of our monks, who is a bonsai expert, examined the tree carefully. He sees life and its wondrous possibilities in all things. This monk chooses to remain anonymous. But if you ever come here and bring with you an ailing plant (or heart), he will rise with joy from his obscurity. He always does when someone is in need.

He gently teased the soil at the base of the trunk and with a cry of delight found the tiniest green leaf sprouting just at the soil line. "Yes, yes," he said, as if he had just discovered gold, "This tree will be fine."

I was amazed. I never would have given the little tree a chance. It turns out that the tree was a wedding anniversary gift that a friend of Mary's had given to his wife, and she apparently lacked a green bonsai thumb.

The tree is now taller, full of leaves, healthy branches and new growth. It has grown to twice the size it was when Mary first brought it. All this has come from that tiny speck of green and a monk's vigilant and tender care.

I like to think that our lives are sometimes like that tree. We may look at ourselves and all we may see are dead ends, withered possibilities, shrunken prospects, and dried and shriveled hopes. But at the bottom of such decay may well be the tiniest movement of life. It is from that mere point that we should pray.

Plants need time and patience to develop and grow. We can easily give them that. What is more difficult is giving our weaknesses over to God and allowing God to love us just as we are. All growth, like that little tree, starts from the smallest possibilities and spreads upward and outward to genuine sources of life. Human life is no different. Our deepest hunger is for God, who is our light, our sustenance, our very food.

A CHANGE OF BEAT

One of the first monks I met here was Brother William. He worked and lived in the retreat house where I stayed for two weeks during the initial interview process before entering the monastery. I would get up earlier than I had to and write or read in the retreat house dining room. William was always there ahead of me, making the coffee and readying the place for the day's guests.

During that time William told me a few things about himself. He was a Franciscan and served in Peru before entering the Trappists. He grew up in New Jersey, as did I. And he plays the saxophone. He told me that he played in clubs all over the New York metropolitan area and astounded me when he said that he played clubs in Newark. I told him that must have been before my time.

I found out later that William put away his saxophone when he entered religious life. I sense, though he never told me, that the instrument represented for him a way of life, even perhaps a way of love, that he freely chose to leave behind when he became a monk. Looking at him sing in choir, I can tell that he loves music. He walks in measured steps, and there is something harmonious about the way he is so open and friendly with people.

I suppose that any life choice demands a parting of ways, a series of sacrifices that must be made if we are to move ahead and follow our heart's true desire. Any given day is filled with such choices. Things are done and even said at the expense of other, equally good, things.

I like to observe William's joy and real zest as he goes through his days here. His affection for life is contagious. At this point, it can be said that he chose to follow the call of a different drum and attuned his heart to a new song.

In the process of doing so, I do not think he has ever missed a beat.

THE PATHMAKER

Early Christianity was called the Way, and we are called to follow it and to help others do the same.

To walk the Way is to walk in goodness. It is to live your life for others. Yet we can easily get lost until a fellow traveler helps us along.

There are large wooded areas at the monastery where people rarely venture. The floor of the forest is hidden beneath a deep layer of leaves, brush and pine needles. In some areas, the only paths are those that have been worn and made firm by the many deer who feel much at home here.

One day, I was walking in such an area and up ahead of me I saw movement. It was Gerard, one of our monks, walking through the forest. He did not see me, and I did not want to startle him. I slowed a bit and then noticed that he was dragging something behind him. It looked to be some sort of heavy mat that had a rope attached to it. He was stooped as he slowly moved ahead of me.

Gerard spotted me and then smiled and stopped, waiting for me to catch up to him. As I approached him, I saw that the mat was actually made of a metal mesh. I asked him if he wanted me to carry it for a while and he said no, that he was making a path through the woods. And sure enough, I saw that where he had dragged the mat, there was a leveling of the grass and the leaves. "Others may want to walk here," he said. "This will make it easier." And that was that. We chatted for a while, and then went our separate ways. I headed back to the monastery buildings, and Gerard advanced into the woods, dragging his little pathmaker behind him.

Henry James, when asked what three things he felt to be the necessary qualities for a good and full life, responded by saying, "The first is kindness, and the second is kindness, and the third is kindness." I do not think Gerard has ever had to think much about choosing any other options. Everything he does has a genuine touch of kindness to it, from his smile, to his concern for others, to the way he walks.

Every now and then while walking in the forest, I come across a path that seems to have been laid down before me by magic. Then I think of Gerard, moving gently through the woods, making a path for others. I do not think that he ever told anyone else what he does, but a lot can be learned from just watching a man like him.

CALLING MY NAME

We have a house here at the monastery reserved for the families and friends of the monks. It is an old, beautiful house situated on a lake and has all the comforts of home. Our families and friends come from far and wide and stay for several days, and those days are always filled with catching up on family news and above all the joy of simply being with family.

Departures, however, are always difficult for me. My mom, sister and brothers live great distances from here, and saying good-by is always a heavyhearted experience.

After one such departure, I needed time alone and went back into the empty guest house. I sat in a large comfortable rocking chair and turned on the television set. We normally do not watch TV in the cloister, and it felt strange listening to disembodied voices and perfectly timed sound and laughter. There was a comedy on and in my empty-hearted state the routines seemed canned and predictable. I was lonely and missed the presence of others, but I did not want to leave just then to go looking for someone back at the main building. I still needed time to savor the fresh and lingering love and presence of my family.

Suddenly I heard a knock at the back door and then heard it open and my name called. I immediately recognized the voice as Mark's, one of our monks. The simple call of my name from a friend was in sharp contrast to the anonymous sound emanating from the television. Mark's voice gave me a deep sense of being called back to myself and to the world of friendship, care and commitment to one another that is our community.

I called to Mark to come in, and he entered the room with a warm smile and sat in a chair next to me. He said that he had driven down to the main gate and said good-by to my family. I was touched by his thoughtfulness and told him so. I was equally moved by his returning to the guest house, where he seemed to know I would be—and in need of friendship. The hour or so that we spent talking that night had a sacred quality to it—two solitudes that touched in a way that needed no explanation to verify it.

When Mark called my name, I awoke once again to the goodness of my life here. I had a profound sense that night that I never really said good-by to the best of what my family is about. In the person of Mark and those like him, I know I have here in the monastery what is most real about my family. We seek one another with a love and presence that is more genuine than the entire world of mass media and high-tech communication.

NATURE'S COURSE

I had been working right near the tree for several weeks, and I did not see the nest. It was small, hardly noticeable. It could have easily fit in a human hand. What brought my attention to it was the sound of baby birds chirping. Careful not to disturb them, I moved close to the tree and was surprised that the nest had been built at eye level. Had I wanted to, I could have easily reached in and touched the baby birds.

As I stood there, the mother bird hesitated to return to the nest. She monitored my movement from a telephone wire a stone's throw away. Only after I moved what she considered a safe distance away did she fly to the nest and feed her young. I counted four little chicks, their tiny fuzzy heads frantically bobbing up and down as soon as they sensed that their mother was near.

I returned to the area near the tree each day for several weeks after discovering the small brood and was fascinated by the vigilant care the mother lavished on the four baby birds. She made constant trips back and forth to the nest, returning each time with morsels of food.

The chicks grew rapidly. By simply watching the routine of their mother I picked up some small lessons in nature and nurture that I had never known. The mother would not come to the nest if I stood nearby, and if I drew too close she would chirp wildly. Not wanting to cause any undue alarm, I would gently back off, freeing her from worry. I also noticed that the chicks instinctively grew quiet, and even cowered to the bottom of the nest, when I drew close.

One morning, I approached the nest and was startled to see that it was empty. By then I well knew the distinctive sound of the young birds, and I soon heard, from several directions not at all far from me, their plaintive chirps. I stepped back and kept myself at a safe distance, just waiting to see what would transpire.

It was not long before I realized what had happened. The young had simply reached a point in their development when they could venture on their own from the nest. I was able to see all four of them, in various branches hopping distances away from the nest. One young chick, however, had fallen and was chirping wildly from a handful of brush not far from where I was standing. Fearing that it would soon fall prey to one of the cats that frequented the area, I moved toward it and gingerly grasped the little bird, but as soon as I took it into my hands both the baby and its mother began to chirp frantically. I knew immediately that I had overstepped a natural boundary, so I placed the small creature on the ground. It hobbled off toward the nearest shelter it could find, which happened to be the base of an enormous tree. The other three chicks were silent, and as I got far enough away the mother bird flew to her wandering chick and fed it.

Things seemed to go well for the rest of that day, though I noticed that the chick that I had picked up was in an orbit of its own, seemingly unable to get back to the safer refuge of its siblings, who had kept to the branches of the tree where they were born.

The next day, the young chick was not to be found. The other three were still safe in the tree, and I watched their mother make numerous flights back and forth to them. Not once did I see her stray from her trips to that tree. I never again was able to account for the missing and almost surely dead bird. I looked for it and never found a trace of it. As the weeks passed, I watched the brood brave ever-widening horizons, their mother continuing to feed them all the while. One day, however, they must have reached a point where they were able to fend for themselves, since all that was left of their lives was an empty nest.

How I wish I had not interfered with nature's course. Perhaps that little bird would have somehow made it to where its siblings now fly with abandon. It may seem like a paltry thing for me to fret over, since nature is, I know, harsh to begin with. But my reaching out that morning seemed to seal the fate of a creature so small, innocent and dependent.

Thinking of life writ large, I realize that being human invariably involves so many decisions, indeed, so many risks—and that many of these risks can involve loss. Perhaps love is the most intricate and most exacting of these risks. When we give from our deepest self there are no sure maps and no guarantees as to how it will all turn out.

Perhaps my tale of the little bird is too simple and worthy of dismissal. But I believe that seemingly small things bear within them the capacity to teach lessons of great magnitude. I can only ask forgiveness from what slips through my hand and be grateful for whatever I may help along the way.

At times it is difficult to be vigilant and tender toward all that is small and seemingly insignificant, yet life abounds with such things. Perhaps their plenitude exists because we are so slow to learn.

ON WATERING PLANTS

One summer, I was assigned to water plants each day, four hours a day, for just over four months. I worried a lot about keeping my mind active as I watched umpteen gallons of water splash over the plants. I sang songs to myself, mused over my past, thought about my plans for the future, tried hard to take my task one day at a time. I was trying to think my way into meaningfulness.

I thought about people all over the world who were doing more relevant, and obviously more successful things, than I. In many ways, I felt that I was wasting time, that there were surely more important things that I could be doing with my life.

I felt like a human siphon. Water was passing through me and not much else. I experienced very little fulfillment or genuine pleasure. I was watering plants, period. What's more, people looked at me and did not even wave or otherwise acknowledge my existence. Something about that particular job smeared me onto the canvas of oblivion.

I never got angry at the plants. It was not their fault. As a matter of fact, I soon began to take to heart the fact that they somehow needed me. I soon found myself talking to them, worrying about them, checking each of them for signs of illness and fatigue. I wondered if they possessed any sort of consciousness—if they ever grew jealous when their neighbors received more water or a better place in the sun. I wondered if they felt sadness as they lost their leaves or even their lives. All these things wandered through my mind as I carefully aimed the hose and allowed the clear and cool water to gush, splash, squirt and spray.

Each plant required a different method of water allocation and delivery. I learned this as time went on. I also watched for soil levels and whether fertilizer was needed. I looked out for harmful bugs and worms. I soon knew the difference between good bugs and not-so-good bugs. There were many little tricks that I picked up as the days grew into weeks and then months. I fancied myself something of a watering expert by summer's end—no diploma, no certificate, no added line on my curriculum vita, but an expert just the same.

And something good did come out of it.

That something has to do with the human need to engage in seemingly useless activity...and to do so on purpose. It concerns doing things without a hope of getting something back. I now realize that such activity is how life itself thrives and blooms.

We have to keep an eye open for where such activity occurs, however, for it is almost invisible. It blends in with the scenery as it goes about tending to its daily tasks.

Just as the monastery plants would have died without the water I delivered, we too would die without all that gushes continuously around us: goodness, patience, kindness, hope, human warmth—given so freely by so many, usually with little or no notice.

THREADS OF GRACE

I went for a walk earlier this morning in the monastery woods. It was a cool day and this morning was particularly beautiful. The sun shone through the hundreds of trees in the forest, and countless spider webs glistened, strewn between branches no matter where I looked. It was as if thousands of fairies had been busy throughout the night, stringing strands of precious silver thread from branch to branch, for no other reason than to add more beauty for me to observe.

As the sun rose, however, the strands vanished from sight. The delicate threads need the bright rays of morning for visibility.

I think of grace as spider webs that are always present in our lives. Every so often—say in a brilliant and clear moment like this morning—we can see how beautiful everything is, connected by glistening strands, dancing and swaying all around us. With less light, the grace remains, but we have to look a bit harder for it. And in the times of total darkness, we must make an act of faith that grace still abounds.

CAT GREETINGS

His name is BC, short for Barn Cat. We found him as a kitten, and he has made the large bonsai barn his home. He is orange and with his winter coat looks fat and fluffy.

Walking down to the barn yesterday morning, I was whistling some forgettable tune to myself. Out of the corner of my eye I saw movement, and there was BC bouncing across the field toward me. He was meowing as he trotted along, glad to see a familiar face after a long and perhaps lonesome night in the field, though he prefers it out there and has found a way to exit the barn whenever he feels a pang of hunger or wanderlust (or maybe just plain old lust).

BC came right up to me and brushed against my legs. I leaned over and petted him and was happy to see him. I thought how such a mundane little ritual as a cat greeting a man can lift one's spirits. I realized that much of creation greets us daily. There is a welcoming sense to nature, despite its occasional harshness and indifference to those who are passing through.

Maybe there is something to learn from the gentle brush of a cat or a branch or a breeze.

BC was glad to see me. It is as simple as that. I made it a point to remember to express the same gratitude to those who crossed my path that day.

THE MONASTIC VOCATION

Vaun was a teacher of socially disadvantaged kids before he entered the Monastery of the Holy Spirit. His religious name here is Chaminade.

I like to hear Chaminade talk of his teaching experience. He speaks with fondness of the kids he knew over the years and still worries about them. He wanted them to have a chance at a good and better life and knew the importance of education. I sense that he must have been a wonderful presence in a classroom. He is a very open person, warmly attracted and attractive to others.

Diversity does not seem to bother Chaminade. He moves easily through difference, not trying to reduce it to a singularity of any sort. In his quiet way, he allows people to be themselves. Perhaps that is why I find him such a pleasure to be with.

We wrap pots together in our bonsai department and have the chance to talk a lot as we select pots and prepare them for shipment. As the pots are wrapped in plastic bubble wrap and placed in boxes, our conversation touches upon all sorts of things. I like to get Chaminade laughing—he has a good laugh, a laugh that comes from deep inside of him, from that place where his students still live and claim his concern.

One day, he told me how much he misses teaching. He has mentioned this before, but on that particular day he seemed especially worried and sad. It is a struggle for most monks, wondering if we would be doing some more tangible good elsewhere—in Chaminade's case back in a classroom.

That was the question he was posing and for which I have no easy or sure answer. Can one remain in a cloistered monastery and serve by simply being what one feels called to be? Chaminade imparts something to everyone with his smile, his integrity, his fidelity to seeking truthfulness. Is he not a teacher? Does teaching necessarily involve a building and classrooms, a student body and faculty, taxes and tuition? Or is the essence of teaching the learned and the unlearned, with some sense of reciprocity between the two?

I looked at Chaminade. I know that he teaches by all that he is. He teaches of the God who loves him and somehow has beckoned him to this monastic life—to wonder, to seek, to refine, and to share who he is and what he knows.

A friend once gave me a chalice on which is engraved: "You give much and know not at all that you give." I think the words are those of Kahlil Gibran. We never know much about how others see us; what it is that we give to them. I doubt that it is of any matter to see ourselves as others do. Maybe in God's plan it is more important to see what others give, what their lives teach us.

Maybe that is the secret of the monastic vocation.

THE ART OF WASTING TIME

Our culture thrives on doing. Idle time is easily seen as nonproductive. Many people experience guilt if they find that they have time on their hands and cannot fill it with something. I have often thought how youngsters these days are so caught up in an adolescent version of the rat race, having their days so compartmentalized. Everything is planned for them. Much of the spontaneity and frivolity that should be part and parcel of "play" has been neatly ordered and packaged by well-intentioned adults whose own lives are burdened by all sorts of schedules and routines.

I suggest that we all learn the art of wasting time. But please, don't plan it. Just do it.

I used to like sitting on the front steps of my home in the evening during the warm summer months. I sat there and listened and watched and wondered. I liked the sounds of laughter, of people talking, of a late-afternoon breeze as it caressed the trees. I liked to watch the passing cars, and every so often the evening was graced with the beauty of a full and rich moon, with clouds chasing each other across the sky's surface. I looked at the stars and contemplated their beauty and unimaginable distance. I may have been wasting time, but I do not regret it.

In the stillness of many a summer night, the memory of that street where I lived and the heavens above me become one, and I am where they meet.

What, then, do monks do? Some say that we do nothing. Absolutely nothing.

Others say that in doing so, we are involved in absolutely everything.

There is a great porch at the rear of our monastery church. I go there on summer nights and sit and do nothing. The shooting stars above Conyers are a glory to behold. There is always an extra chair.

CONYERS SPRING

We had a glorious spring this year. There were many cool days, which brought with them a good balance of sun and rain. So much comes to life in the spring: the trees, new plants, the grasses and shrubs, and of course all the animals. And here in the South, the night air is filled with the sounds of millions of insects. By early summer, baby birds, deer, kittens and squirrels are plentiful. This spring I had the joy of watching on many a morning as a mama turkey and her eight plump chicks fed near the forest's edge behind the barn where I read.

All the above is just what one monk sees and hears. I can only imagine all the life around me that I cannot see, yet I know it teems there. Spring springs to life all on its own. As a Zen master once said, "Sit back and the spring comes."

The earth renews itself through its seasonal cycles in ways that we are only beginning to fathom. The earth is a living system—it heals, renews, balances and replenishes; it dies and rises again.

We humans are a living part of this mystery. We, too, have seasons of decline and renewal, times that are spiritually lean and times of abundant harvest.

To behold a spring day in Conyers is indeed wonderful. To entrust my life to the God who creates such beauty here is a privilege.

NOTE BY NOTE

Being a cantor in a monastic choir can be a humbling lesson in getting lost and being found. There are many things to learn when one starts out as a novice in the *schola* here—the proper notes, cadence, and page numbers; who does which response when; when to sing and when to remain silent. These things must be remembered all at once, and it can get unnerving to say the least.

I have floundered many times. What both amazed and heartened me were my fellow monks, who bailed me out and kept the chant going as smoothly as if nothing had happened. I soon learned that there is an instinctive willingness among the monks to pitch in and retrieve a wandering or lost note (or novice). It took me a good while to trust that larger sense of organic care that exists in the choir and, as I have learned, all through the life here. My realization of its presence grew in proportion to my need for it. We monks strive to live (and sing) for God and one another. Where one monk may be weak, the strength or charity of another finds what is lost or wayward and cares for that loss by love, prayer, or the right and perfectly timed note.

Being a human gathering, a monastery is far from a perfect system. We do not make up a perfect body, but that does not matter. Perfection is not what monastic life is about. On more than one occasion, when my notes (or my charity) have gone flat and sour, I have been sung or simply loved right back into the music of the life here.

LEARNING THE ROPES

One of my daily jobs in the monastery is the ringing of the church bells for the Angelus and Compline. It may sound like an easy enough job, but I found out the first time I did it that it would take me more than a few times to get it right. There is an art to pulling the long rope just right and doing it at the required pace and with the proper amount of yank.

My first few days at the task were rocky. My timing was way off and in my nervousness I pulled the rope an extra time or two. The bell also tolled flat. For ten days thereafter, one of the veteran monks stood right in front of me as I tolled the bell, coaching me and encouraging me. With his help and patience, I graduated to solo and the bells now ring loud and clear. Eventually, I will be showing someone else the ropes.

One discovers oneself through the delight of learning to love and be loved. Teachers abound—those gifted and generous people who love well and teach us to ring the symphonies of our own bells. The learning is in the doing and persisting—through days and sometimes years—until loving is as easy and as natural as ringing a bell.

THE HEART OF TEXAS

I was in Texas once, many years ago, for the wedding of a friend. I did not see much of the state, certainly nowhere near what I needed to get a feel for the place.

I was recently given a taste of Texas once again, however, and I got there through a song.

Not long ago, Brother Tom, our cantor, invited me down to the monastery guest house to spend the evening with his sister Mary and their dad, Al. They were here for a few days from San Antonio. They are the kind of people who welcome you into their lives with ease and warmth. After just a little while with them, I felt that I had known them all my life.

We sat around the kitchen table, relaxing and sharing stories. The sun had gone down, but I could still see some ducks gliding softly across the lake just outside the window of the kitchen. Mary, in the course of the conversation, asked Tom if he remembered a particular song that they used to sing together as kids. Tom slowly sang the first few verses of a Burl Ives song that I had never heard before. Tom has a beautiful voice, and Mary and Al smiled as they joined in. Mary asked Tom if he remembered one other song, and then another, and another. She recalled snatches of lyrics and a bit of melody, and Tom was able to immediately offer the rest of the song. In between the songs, the three of them laughed and reminisced about the circumstances surrounding each song. It was as if each tune were a line thrown into a sea of memory that pulled a story of their lives to the surface—warm and glistening and very much alive.

A few of songs were about Texas. All of them were about love and hope and loss.

Texas will always be a place I visited that night in a Georgia kitchen. I was asked to go there, and indeed I went. Tom's family's easy ways gave me a glimpse of the vastness and wealth of Texas and the warmth of its people. What I saw of Texas that night I loved. It is a wonder to me how a place so big can fit so easily in a human heart and be shared so fully in a matter of hours.

Now I do not have to travel to get to Texas. When Tom sings in the choir, I listen to him and am easily carried back again to that night in the kitchen…and from there to Texas. The cloister makes such travel possible. It is not so much a place as a state of mind.

SACRED GRAVES

It lies hidden in the woods, not far off a path that winds its way through the forest that surrounds the monastery. The woods are in the monastic enclosure, so we monks are the only ones who wander through it these days. We seem to be the only ones who know where the cemetery is.

One of the older monks told me about it and showed me the way. I have gone there by myself many times to pray.

It is a slave cemetery.

It is a sacred place, a hollowed place. The remains of the slaves lie buried beneath the forest, the ground covered with leaves and rocks and dead branches. The only things that mark the graves as such are small, rough stones that look as if they were just thrown about. You have to observe carefully to discern that they have a pattern and that the earth before each stone is slightly sunken. There are no crosses or legible markers of any kind. The graves have been untouched and largely unknown, except by the monks, for more than one hundred years.

I walked down there on Good Friday and thought of the lives whose remains lay beneath me, forever lost to history and human memory. I prayed to the God who cried and sweat and suffered with them, to the same God whose Son died and lay buried in an unmarked, borrowed grave.

The woods are silent, save for the sound of the wind, the songs of the birds, the hum and cadence of the insects.

I pray that I learn to hear the silent cries of those who lie there in peace, in the womb of an earth that has been seeded with the life of the One who shall call them to rise again.

ONE HAND REACHING OUT
TO ANOTHER

One month after my father passed away, I preached at a Memorial Mass celebrated for him at the monastery. It was a very hard thing for me to do, and I considered ducking the invitation. I wanted to share with my fellow monks some thoughts about Dad, a man I loved very much whom they had never met. But the pain of losing him was still deep and fresh, and I did not want to get overly emotional.

Toward the end of the homily, the combination of my love for my father and the love I have been so freely given by the monks here at Conyers welled up in my heart. I stared at the few notes I had and started to cry. I had reached that place where there is only wordless mystery. I bowed my head, folded my notes, and proceeded slowly back to my place in the choir. As I passed Abbot Bernard, I felt his hand reach out and take mine and gently squeeze it.

Emmanuel means "God with us." I do not believe that God exists apart from our need to reach out and touch those spaces that ache in each other. There is no "God not with us."

Dom Bernard grasped my hand in human solidarity, and as I sat down I remembered what I tearfully told Dad as he lay dying and asked me what I thought would happen to him. I told him to try to be at peace and pray that God would take him by the hand and bring him to his eternal home.

Emmanuel, our joy and our very life, we pray that you give

us the hope that is your presence. Help us to reach out to each other with our hands...and our hearts.

KAREN'S RESOLUTION

Being organized is not a strong trait of mine. I have tried many times to become a more disciplined person, but I have as many times lapsed back into the same old routines. Paperwork piles up. Jobs take on a scattered quality. I plan one thing and end up doing something else. I make lists and misplace them. I even bought a book on how to stop procrastinating and put off reading it.

I was in a bit of a funk not too long ago about all this as I walked down to the bonsai barn, where we store all our bonsai pots for shipment. Karen, who works there, greeted me cheerily as I walked in.

Karen champions the bright side of things. She paid me a few kind words that so lifted my spirits that I once again made myself a promise to organize myself just a little bit better.

For a modest start, I promised to write a little bit each day, no matter how I felt, and to make one list of ten things to get done.

This resolution has helped a lot. I am writing each day and have only two more things to accomplish on my list. Item nine is to make a new list and item ten is to write this little essay on Karen's kind words. Ten has been a joy.

Number nine I'll do later.

ANNE'S KITTENS

The voice was so soft I barely heard it. It took a while for me to discern where it was coming from as I moved slowly in its direction. It was a late-summer evening and I was walking on the road behind our retreat house. In the light coming from the back of the retreat house porch I saw her. It was Anne, who works and lives in the retreat house. I could see her on the porch, leaning over just a bit, but she did not see me.

I kept walking slowly, not wanting to frighten or disturb her. Then I saw movement at her feet. I counted three kittens, inching their way toward her, being enticed by the soothing quality of her voice. She had set out a dish of leftovers and was trying to win them over. Finally, she looked up and saw me, smiled and waved. I waved back and continued on my way.

I, too, felt soothed and assured by Anne's voice that night. I know her to be a kind and caring woman, and I was moved by her solitude that night. She was alone, but she was calling to the kittens to befriend them and share her goodness with them.

We assume that humans are the only ones who truly hear and speak. True, our hearing and speaking are different from other creatures, and some say that we are of a higher order because of such faculties. But that night I heard around me myriad sounds—crickets and frogs, ducks and geese, owls, dogs and cats. All were communicating something and were surely heard and responded to by others of like kind or species.

Yet as far as I know only one species among them tried to

befriend another. Anne's voice, in that sense, stood out from all the rest.

Perhaps that is one of the finest possibilities of human language—that we can speak in the hope of befriending all living things.

PATTI'S COMPLIMENT

Earlier this morning I saw Patti, who works in our retreat house. I had given her a batch of essays to read a while back, and she told me this morning how much she liked them. I was a bit embarrassed because I suppose I really do not think about my writing all that much. I thanked Patti and told her that her opinion meant a lot to me.

Later, I thought back on what Patti said. She is a warm and friendly person, and I admire her ease with people and how readily she shares her goodness in concrete ways. She accomplishes this every day by doing and saying and loving. I admire that.

And so I write about Patti, taking care with my words. For doing and saying and loving is what I most want to write about.

THE BEAUTIFUL FLOWER

In a garden on the monastery grounds stands a large fountain. In front of the fountain once grew a large flower, the name of which I never knew. I would go to the garden very early in the morning, just before dawn, and at that early hour the petals of the flower were always closed. As I sat there, the sun would slowly rise and I would watch the flower carefully, hoping to see it open. It always stayed closed, however, and I soon would go back inside and forget about it.

If I returned several hours later, though, the flower would invariably be opened as fully as possible—so much so that its outer petals, almost the size of a sheet of paper, looked to be in danger of falling to the ground.

When I returned again later in the afternoon as the sun was setting, those same petals would have slowly risen to enclose the smaller petals and hide them once again for another night.

Erected right over the fountain is a sand casting of a lamb pierced with a sword. It is the ancient symbol of the Paschal Lamb, the Risen Christ—a simple and quite beautiful work of art. As I sat before the flower and the Lamb for so many hours, I imagined the flower to be humanlike, opening slowly to the presence and immediacy of the light and warmth of the sun and folding in upon itself as shelter from the cold and darkness.

It is God who gave life and beauty to that flower each day, and each night the Lamb silently graced the darkness of the garden as a reminder that life is present even when we might seek to hide from it.

MEGHAN'S MACARONIS

There is a place deep in our woods at the monastery where I sit and read and write. It is just the right size to accommodate me and the few things that I bring with me.

I am never really alone in this place. My friends for that part of the day are the animals and insects that live there in abundance. Birds and frogs, ants and wandering cats, salamanders, snakes, squirrels, and so many other "creeping things and winged fowl," as the psalm goes. The trees are tall, creating a canopy high above the forest floor that offers generous shade in the warmer months. And in the winter, with the branches bereft of their leaves, sunshine pours through. It is a place that truly speaks to my heart and soul in a language richer than human speech.

Indeed, the finest of human words, those of the poet, try to capture the language of nature in the medium of human letters, rhyme, syntax. Yet how to speak the wind, or phrase the sun, or turn the song of a bird into consonants and vowels? When I raise my head from my book or paper and feel all that is around me, I try to let it speak as only nature can.

A few days ago I was in my spot. It was early morning, and I was reading when I noticed a sound that I had not heard before. All around me was a soft crackling sound, not unlike the falling of snow on dry leaves in early winter. It was a clear morning, the sun was still rising, and the sound baffled me. As pervasive as it was, I could not determine what was causing it. Then I heard something hitting the pages of my book, and looking at the book that lay open on my knees I saw tiny flecks of brown. I picked one of them up and holding it close to my eyes saw that it was a seed. The trees around me—all of the same type of fir—were filled with cones that had opened and whose seeds were falling to the ground. It was a shower of new and promised life, the first beginnings of great things to become. The forest was replenishing itself.

I thought about how everything seemed so harmonious and connected that morning. Of course this kind of rebirth happens all the time, but I had never experienced it before as intently as that morning, when the seeds were literally falling on my head.

Saint Bernard of Clairvaux wrote long ago that "our works do not pass away; rather, they are scattered like temporal seeds of eternity. The fool will be astonished when he sees a great harvest shooting up from a little seed—good or bad harvest according to the different quality of the sowing. . . . So, practice random kindness and senseless acts of beauty."

I had Bernard's very words in my pocket the morning I heard the seeds falling. The words are printed on a card we give to guests who spend time in our retreat house.

I remember a meal I had with my sister Mary, her husband, Brian, and their family when I visited them in Switzerland one time. Mary had made cheese macaroni, and across from me sat my niece Meghan, who was then three years old. On a red plastic plate, which was at eye level with her on the table, Meghan had arranged her macaronis with great care, using her fingers to situate them just so. I can still see her face as she looked at me, giggled, and ate the macaronis one by one with a look of delight that is rare this side of Eden. Her pleasure was manifold: she loved the macaroni, loved her decorative style, loved me for coming to visit, loved eating without a fork, and obviously loved being three years old and having not a care in the world.

Not too long ago I reminded Meghan, now in her twenties, about that evening. Giggling in much the same way and taking a strand of blond hair from her eye in exactly the same gesture that she did back then, she said that she did not remember.

But I remember. I wonder how often Mary and Brian did little things for her like preparing that macaroni meal—a thousand, a hundred thousand, a million times? Like seeds dropped long ago, such little things have grown and now have a life of their own.

THE BLUE RADIO

I once had the smallest of radios—actually it was what was called a crystal set—made of blue plastic. It was about half the size of a shoe box and had just two dials. I had ordered it from the back of a comic book, and it was one of the first things that I had ever purchased through the mail.

I must have been thirteen or fourteen years old at the time. The radio cost only a few dollars, which seemed like a lot of money to me back then. I so looked forward each day for the brown UPS truck.

One day, the small package arrived. The radio was wrapped, with special assembly directions for the all-important crystal. Putting it together was very easy. There were only a few pieces—the plastic body, an earphone and the crystal. To my delight, it really worked.

The crystal was capable of picking up only AM stations. It would be a few more years before FM became the more popular frequency for rock 'n' roll. Each night, I lay in bed with the small earpiece all but glued to my ear. I put it on my pillow and listened as I fell asleep. The copper wire sometimes came loose, but if I jiggled the wire just right, I was able to pick up such stations as WABC, WMCA and WINS, the three main rock stations at the time in the New York metropolitan area.

I remember one night in particular. A blizzard had struck the New York area, and it was a major one. As I lay in my bed that night, listening to music as the wind howled and the night sky was furious with snow, I became aware of the paradoxical stillness that a blizzard brings. Everything in the world had stopped, as far as I was concerned, except for the wind and the snow and the music.

I felt a sense of awe that through a wire and blue plastic I was connected to the world, in spite of the storm. It did not matter that the radio was small and inexpensive. For the comfort it brought me that night, I would not have traded it for the fanciest radio in the world.

Something so simple gave me incredible pleasure. As the years passed, my little crystal radio was replaced with large and more expensive sets that had rows of lights and dials. As much as I enjoyed later models, however, the innocence and pleasure of that first simple blue set contained a magic I never recaptured.

That was forty years—and so many songs—ago. I now live in a cloister, where there are no radios or televisions (and no snowstorms, either). Not long ago, while lying in bed one night waiting for sleep to come, I thought about that little blue radio and the simple but rich pleasures it brought me. Looking back, I think that it served a purpose that is becoming clearer to me as I pass my days and nights in monastic peace. In a sense, the little blue radio is still communicating something to me after all these years.

These days I must fine tune the receptor that is my heart. And on those nights that God seems far away, I need to jiggle the connection just a bit.

GRACE IS EVERYWHERE

I was recently home to visit my mother, who lives in Covington, Louisiana, in an assisted-care facility called Christwood. Mom has her own apartment, and the place is beautiful in many ways. She has friends in abundance, regular visits from my brothers and sisters, and her good health, except for an advanced case of macular degeneration that has left her legally blind.

I was there for two weeks, and since the apartment is small I slept on the couch in the living room. It was comfortable. Since coming to the monastery I have become used to a smaller bed on which to sleep.

I drove to Louisiana from Conyers, and the ride afforded me a chance to acclimate myself to returning to the hustle and bustle of American culture. It had been just over two years since I had last been home, and that was for Dad's funeral.

I was surprised, as the miles piled up on the odometer of the rented car, how accustomed I had become to the routine of monastic life and being pretty much in one place for most of the time. There is nothing particularly religious or sacred about that. What happens, though, is that the absence of most distractions makes room for the fullness of awareness. The monastic life—the smells of forest and incense, the sounds of bells, the rush of the wind, the cadence of the rain—seeps deeply into one's very pores. I experience these things with an attention that I never had before. It all adds up to a daily invitation that comes from all around me to be attentive, to listen, to see, to respond.

Monastic life grounds me. I know I am more at peace inside the monastery than outside. I also know that the monastery environment is not artificial. Human life is lived in the cloister: monks work, hope, suffer, celebrate and wonder like everyone else. What seems to me to be the biggest difference "in here"—as opposed to "out there"—is our commonly shared attempt to live as simple a life as possible.

Before I came to Conyers, I could easily plug my attention into a lot of things: television, the stereo, billions of words in countless conversations, running hither and yon with all sorts of things to do. That can happen in monastic life, too. A monk can lose himself in busyness. He can live from day to day or month to month and not take notice of all that is around him. But that has not been my experience.

Might I say that a Trappist monastery is a place where heart and memory become more expansive? They become free to roam terrains that are more natural to them. I have found in the nearly four years that I have been a monk that I have had to learn to pray in ways that I never did before. I have simply been given more of myself to deal with.

My memory now reaches far and wide. It seems as if it is looking for something, as if it has a life and intent all its own. It brings things back to me that I had long forgotten. A few days ago, I thought of a dog my family once had, Rusty, who would bound into the woods and come back with the oddest of things, a stick or a ball that had been thrown there weeks or years before. My memory seems to function like Rusty did. It goes off on its own and comes back with things I wasn't even looking for. The monastery has exposed my memory to a wide-open field—

my past—and for the first time in my life it is free to run and retrieve what it fancies. I am trying to understand what to do with what it brings back, and writing helps.

As soon as I drove out of the car-rental place, I could immediately feel the pull of American culture around me. There were so many things demanding my attention—music on the radio, news broadcasts, advertisements, billboards. I was aware of the two-week limit of my stay, and I wanted to give Mom my undivided attention. I took her shopping, to the hairdresser, Clovis, to the drugstore, to visit relatives. We had quiet times, too—dinners and breakfasts and lunches when it was just the two of us. Yet even during those times, I yearned for a stillness that seemed to evade me. My mind and heart were always racing faster than I could understand. I did not say anything to Mom other than a comment or two on how quickly time goes.

One morning not very long into my stay, I awoke to the sound of a man's voice coming from the room where Mom has her television and her reading machine. I quietly got up and walked the few steps into the room, and there was Mom sitting as close as she could before the television set, watching a televised Mass that is broadcast daily from New Orleans. The celebrant that morning was the retired Archbishop of New Orleans, Phillip Hannon. It was his voice that I responded to; it is very distinctive and calm. Mom had her rosary beads in her hand. She could not see me, since I was behind her. I sat down quietly and prayed the rest of the Mass with her. Suddenly, I felt more at home than I could have ever imagined.

Praying quietly along with Mom, I felt connected to her, to those with whom she lives, to my sisters and brothers, to my

Trappist brothers who were then far away. The language of the Mass helped me remember. It called me to something more than I could have found for myself that morning.

Not much later that same morning, still quite early, I went out on the little porch that Mom has at the front of her apartment and watched an elderly man walking his dog. I happened to meet him later, and he told me that he does that every morning. He calls that his "peaceful time." Whether or not he knew it, he expressed the contemplative need in all of us.

It may be tempting to say that a "religious" experience like the Mass is a more refined one than sitting on a porch or walking one's dog, but I think it is best to say that God finds us where we are. We were made to be with God and with one another in peace—walking our dogs, sipping a cup of coffee, praying before a TV set.

Today is early Sunday morning, Low Sunday according to the Psalter, the first Sunday after Easter. It is raining heavily. I wonder if Mom is just getting up from her chair after having watched the televised Mass. Is it raining in Covington, Louisiana? Is that man walking his little dog in the rain?

The dying priest in George Bernanos' *Diary of a Country Priest* sighed as he said, "Grace is everywhere."

Like the rain, we do not make grace fall into our lives. It just comes and comes again.

AFTERWORD

The human being is a creature-in-search whose eternal compass is set to the interminable question "For what?" For what are we really searching in life? Where should we go to seek it? How will we know when we have found it?

The questions ring across time, through great literature, in popular music, behind every major work of art. Every culture, every spirituality, every wisdom figure in every arena of life concentrates on finding the answer to the secret of living, the endpoint of life. Whatever the magnet that draws them on, whatever the tradition that guides them, these seekers walk the same way, they beat a single path, and eventually they come to the same conclusion.

"The meaning of life is to see," as a Chinese proverb teaches. "Listen," the ancient Rule of Benedict instructs. "The real voyage of discovery consists not in seeking new landscapes," the philosopher Marcel Proust writes, "but in having new eyes."

It is not, in other words, so much where we go in life that matters, it is the way in which we immerse ourselves in it, open ourselves to it, see beyond its trappings wherever we are that measures the quality of the journey. This book by James Stephen Behrens is about that same kind of seeking, that same sort of seeing, that same depth of vision.

Grace Is Everywhere expands our vision. It proves the idea that where we are is sacred space, models the apocalypse of dailiness for us, gives us the opportunity to look again at the humdrum, the customary, the bland and the beautiful around us in order to find before our very eyes the edges of the eternal, the gleam of God in the obscure.

This book does two things: it focuses us on the present and it calls us to see beyond it, two elements of crucial importance in a world that is always on its way to somewhere else with nowhere else in mind. As a matter of fact, *Grace Is Everywhere*, written from the Trappist experience of the Rule of Benedict, the guiding spiritual tradition of Behrens' order, is a kind of survey of Benedictine spirituality.

Benedictine monasteries, you see, are not places where visions are expected. Benedictine monasteries are places where visions are considered unnecessary. What is not unnecessary in a Benedictine monastery, however—what is endemic to a Benedictine monastery, indeed—is the development of the contemplative heart, the heart that sees the world as God sees the world.

Monasteries, ironically, are places where what is patently, palpably real—if the contemplation practiced there is real—is considered vision enough. This is a book about Benedictine/ Trappist monasticism that never mentions either the Rule of Benedict or monasticism at all. And that is as it should be. Monastics don't set out to be different from the rest of the world. They set out to be as finely focused of soul as a person can be and still walk the world. They set out to find God in the center of life. They set out to teach the neophyte in the spiritual life how to see what they search for in the very place they're searching for it. They set out to bring insight to what might otherwise be considered dense, in dearth of soul, too conventional to have anything to do with the glut of God.

Grace Is Everywhere presents us with the prototype of the monastic soul. Monasticism centers around six essential measures of human development: community, stewardship, prayer, silence, hospitality and stability. Behrens takes us into this network of monastic values and translates them for us. He shows us how they would look if we ever saw them alive and thriving in our own lives. And in the doing he enables us to look at our own lives again, this time with an eye for the transcendent in the midst of the pedestrian.

When a person begins to look at the world through monastic eyes, everything becomes the stuff of spirituality. Here, for instance, Behrens simply looks at the monastic enclosure in which he lives for models, samples, means of living the qualities that the Rule itself inspires. He talks about simple things, about common things, about the things we take for granted, and in the looking he unmasks for us the sacredness of the mundane. He rides through the monastery property and realizes that all of life is a process. He finds fullness in silence and teaches us that God speaks in the center of those who listen. He says good-by to his family in the monastery guest house and comes to understand that "relationships" are made out of more than blood ties. He talks to visitors and comes to understand that cloister is a quality of mind. He teaches us to see what we're looking at and think about what we're seeing. He leads us all to come to grips with the fact that sanctity is made from the stuff of the ordinary.

Grace Is Everywhere is a disarmingly simple work. At first glance, the book seems to lack a level of substance we've come to associate with erudite presentations of monastic spirituality. A little more thought, on the other hand, and the truth begins to dawn. It seeps into the cellars of the soul until suddenly it becomes clear that the real substance of monastic spirituality may lie in this very simplicity.

Learning to distinguish the real from the imaginary, bringing meaning to life, finding beauty where we have ceased to see may be the missing spiritual discipline of the age. It becomes so easy in an era of plastic relationships, shallow commitments, glittering consumption and human megalomania to substitute sacred rituals for serious reflection, churchgoing for morality, religion for spirituality. Then the meaning of monasticism becomes clear. Then the monastic mindset becomes new again, becomes the cornerstone of a society lost in complexities far beyond their merit. Then, a book like *Grace Is Everywhere* reminds us that life itself, real life, life lived in the commonplace, enriched by reflection and grounded in meaning, may be far simpler than we think.

Joan Chittister, OSB
Mount St. Benedict Monastery
Erie, Pennsylvania

ACKNOWLEDGMENTS

I once asked my sister Mary where she thought vocations (of whatever kind) come from. Without a second's hesitation, she replied, "Everyone." Her words rang true, and I took them to heart.

So, where does a book come from? Everyone, obviously. All the people in my life have made this book possible.

But I would be remiss if I did not express special thanks to Michael Farrell and Tom Fox of the *National Catholic Reporter* who first published my writing and to Greg Pierce and everyone at ACTA Publications who have done so much to bring out my first book. And I must acknowledge Abbot Bernard Johnson, OCSO, and all my brother monks here at Conyers whom I am honored to know and love and with whom I now share my life.

Finally, I offer my deepest appreciation to Dolores Leckey and Sister Joan Chittester, OSB, who believed in me enough to contribute the Foreword and the Afterword to this book.

Good gifts come to everyone from everyone: vocations, books, life itself.

INTERLUDE

The next essay was the very first ever published by James (Jeff) Behrens. It appeared in the *National Catholic Reporter* and was later included in the collection *The Work of Human Hands*.

ANDY'S DINER

The name of the diner was Andy's. It was near a large industrial park, so business was always good, as was the food. The waitresses were friendly and pretty and they knew nearly everyone who came in. Andy's had an attraction for all sorts of people: rich, poor, and in between, neat and sloppy, loud and quiet, varied races, and religious persuasions.

I used to go there alone every morning and find an empty stool near the far end of the counter to better enjoy the parade of humanity.

Most did not know I was a priest. They embodied a richly textured history that unfolded bit by bit over a period of five or so years. I sensed a common something beneath all the variations, some sort of essential goodness that drew people there and seemed waiting to be told.

Andy has since died and the diner is now boarded up. I was honored to offer his funeral Mass. Perhaps his passing and the closing of the diner has prompted me to write of the goodness of Andy and his diner, for they offered more than mere food.

I asked Andy's wife if I could have a small, glass ashtray with the name and address of the diner. It is more valuable to me than all the Waterford in the world. I felt liked there, and in turn truly liked the people who filled the place each morning. They seemed unaware of the wealth of raw and unadorned beauty that their lives and words were.

The place so fascinated me that I went through a period when I would be the first one there, as early as five in the morning. Jack, the short-order cook, went through a meticulous routine of arranging his food and wares for the coming day. He was a friendly man, slender, fast at whatever he had to do. He could handle five or six breakfast orders at once, never losing track of their sequence. I hope he is well these days. His health had started to fail toward the end of my stay. He was missing from Andy's funeral several years ago.

I was pursuing graduate studies and would stop for lunch on my way to class. There was a waitress who worked the lunch-hour shift, young and attractive. One day she told me she noticed my books and school papers. She said she, too, was going to school, trying to get her college degree by going part-time. Waitressing helped her pay tuition and care for her baby. She was divorced and had a difficult time making ends meet. I asked her what she hoped to do after receiving her degree. She said she loved writing and hoped to become a published author.

The next day she brought in one of her essays, a piece about her former husband who was wounded in Vietnam and had suffered flashbacks after returning home. I found her writing so moving, but she never spoke as openly as did her writing.

If I could track her down, I would ask her to write about those years. The most fertile soil is our memories and our loves. Only they can make us grateful. Only they are capable of causing us to feel joy and sorrow. We suffer only from what we have known, from what has deeply touched our being, as those in the diner have touched mine.

———

There was a professional photographer there every morning, in his late thirties, generally healthy looking. He was chatty with Jack and Andy, talking about his family and business. One Monday morning, he was missing from his usual seat. Jack kept his seat empty, not wanting to disappoint him should he arrive.

By Thursday, there was still no sign of him and by then his seat was almost always taken by a newcomer. The next week, the photographer's body was found in his car several miles from the diner. The police judged his death a suicide; he had blown his brains out with a shotgun. He had left the house that morning, the last morning of his life, saying he was going to stop at the diner.

———

Chelsey used to operate a garage across the street from the diner. He was usually the first to arrive after Jack opened for business, shortly after five. He was bald, short, fat, grimy, and smelled like the garage. He was divorced many years ago. It was not hard to tell that he might be a difficult man to get along with.

Chelsey had a repertoire of the funniest but raunchiest jokes I have ever heard. At first, he did not know I was a priest.

Someone must have told him, though, because one morning he acted very sheepish when he came in. He proceeded to tell Jack about the poor condition of the buses.

I felt bad about his change of demeanor, but gradually the conversation between him and Jack became so boring that he again came around to his old and perhaps better self. He died not too long ago. There were no services—he was estranged from his family, and most of his friends had died off. He died alone in his small living quarters attached to the garage.

Andy was a good man. Many poor people traveled by bus from Newark to the many factories in the area. It was not unusual for some of them to stop into the diner and ask Andy for food or money.

He was softhearted. After a lecture on the meager state of his own resources, Andy would ask Jack to prepare a take-out breakfast and would place a five-dollar bill on the little tray before Jack wrapped it up. Those people were often forlorn, forgotten, lonely. They needed someplace where their lives could be given a value simply because their stories and troubles were listened to.

Andy also had an agreement with the warden of a nearby jail. Upon the release of an inmate, Andy told the warden, he would be willing to offer a job in the kitchen until the released person could find a better means of income.

I truly loved the people in that diner, and a generosity of spirit that was so much a part of it. Christmas had such a beautiful meaning there. Andy would decorate the diner with strings of lights and artificial snow from an aerosol can. The diner took on a magical glow and there was a heightened sense of the incarnation.

It was a place in which God himself would have felt at home. Those who frequented Andy's impressed me deeply with their earthiness and their gutsy coping with the harsh realities of life.

I believe God had a special affection for that place. God would have enjoyed every tale of woe and promise and found something of himself in each person there. Their lives were such a potpourri of goodness and wisdom, tempered by the brute numbness of factory labor and the unfairness of the way things are when the lack of power and money afflict human life.

There was something sacramental to it all. Those people gave me something that made me think about and long for the truth and experience of God. I cannot describe the feeling of profound peace I knew on those mornings when I would arrive before dawn, sit at the end of the counter, and meditate. Seeing the milkman come in, then Chelsey, then the local police officer, reminded me how we are all drawn to some essential goodness in life, and that place somehow had it.

—※

Can organized religions learn something from that little diner? Religiosity certainly was not explicitly there in terms of language and ritual, but it was there. What used to get my wheels going was the perception of institutionalized holiness that those people carried with them as apart of the "worldview." Whenever a topic came up that involved the bantering about of God or church, I could pick up feelings of indifference, disappointment, or anger. Institutionalized faith did not mean much to them and had somehow alienated them.

In my heart, I know their feelings were nearly accurate. A significant dimension of the church had removed itself from their experience. They looked at and resented—indeed felt betrayed by—pious attitudes, abstract or removed concerns, clericalism, and at a root a resistance to living in the real world, their world.

They were and are the world of labor, of nonrecognition, of commuters, diners, bus stops: the world that the institutionalized religious concern attempts to convert by exhorting and sermonizing, and yet a world that provides the fresh and raw life from which religious meaning must draw its sustenance for reflection. It is the world from which we all "emerge" and world religious specialists would do well to remember.

—✧

If the church does go bankrupt in terms of personnel and cash, I would suggest that it collapse into diners all over the country. Bishops, remaining priests, gurus, ministers, rabbis, and swamis could find spots at counters across the country and just listen, feel welcome and be friendly.

There would be no dead rectories or manses to return to,

nor would there be the need to return for ceremonies because there would be no congregation. They could go to work, to offices and factories, to schools and garages, to banks and computer terminals and discover one another in diners.

And please, do not seek to impose sacred words or sacred rituals in such places. They are already there. No need to "point out" the religious significance of diners. That seems to function best when left unaddressed.

PART II

Memories of Grace

INTRODUCTION

André Dubus, the acclaimed fiction writer who died recently, once said that when he was writing he often had to leave the book and go for a long walk to allow the remainder of the story to somehow find its own voice.

This method applies to much of life. The more we try to force things, the greater our frustration and disappointment. In many ways, it is often best to step back a bit from the busyness of life and allow things to evolve on their own. The verbal portraits offered in this book are examples of the kinds of thoughts that simply come to me as I live and work and pray in the Cistercian monastery here in Conyers, Georgia, preparing myself to make final vows as a Trappist monk. I did not seek these memories, though I confess that I did hope for them and was glad when they arrived. But I had to work to get the words as nearly right as I could, for the writing of these pieces was like giving linguistic form to whispers—passing somethings that arrived as gifts when I least expected them.

I call these portraits "memories of grace." Writing them was like entering into a freely chosen state of forgetfulness that allowed me to remember. They happened whenever the wheels of my daily grind stopped turning long enough for my memory to move itself into a very different gear—not so much a recollection of past events but an awareness of eternal, transcendent truths that I already somehow "knew" in the very fiber of my being.

We all live by such memories. They have a voice, a warm

voice, something like the voice I imagine God's to be. It is a voice that speaks to each of us from and through where we have been in our life. In a strange, mystical way, it is a voice that asks us to remember where we are going.

A friend recently challenged me to defend the relevance of contemplative life to today's world, specifically to our fast-paced western society. His was not an angry challenge but a seeking one. He trusts me when I tell him that monastic life has something important to offer those outside the cloister, but I have not been able to articulate for him exactly what that something is.

I do not feel comfortable with the classic distinctions between the contemplative and the active life. Such distinctions blur the common and religious humanity that we all share. I do not have "religious" memories here in the monastery, nor am I filled with "pious" thoughts. I admit that officially sanctioned religious language and symbolism abound in this place as in all other religious institutions, but I think the reality that they point to is present everywhere. Religion has no monopoly on the many ways God is at work and at play in the universe.

We Trappist monks live relatively stable lives, which means simply that we promise to stay put in one place and to be there for each other. Like everyone else, however, we make a living, have our ups and downs, find life at times to be very strange, and sometimes wish a lot of things could be different. Yet we try to do the best we can with the silence, solitude and simplicity that we have chosen by spending our days developing memories of grace. Learning and teaching how to do that may be what we contemplatives have most to offer others.

So, I invite you to explore some of my memories of grace, in the hope that you will experience your own.

Come to me, you who desire me,
  and eat your fill of my fruits.
For the memory of me is sweeter than honey,
  and the possession of me sweeter than the honeycomb.

—SIRACH 24:19-20

CHRISTOPHER STREET

The memory is simple and returns to me often and unbidden. It is a delight when it comes and lingers for a while. It seems to like, as I do, the quiet of the woods here at the monastery, for that is where it comes to me with such ease.

The memory is of my mom and dad, sitting in their bedroom before going to bed on a warm summer night. We had a large old home on Christopher Street in Montclair, New Jersey. It was a Dutch colonial, and their bedroom was on the second floor. The rest of us, five sons and two daughters and my grandmother—Dad's mom—were scattered comfortably throughout the rest of the house. Jimmy, my twin, and I slept in a small room on the third floor, which had two closets—as if it was made just for twins. We had our own bathroom at the end of a long hall, and there was a large porcelain tub in there with legs shaped like lions' feet. The toilet was right next to a window that overlooked the back yard, and from that window the Manhattan skyline was visible.

Before going to bed, each of us would stop in and say goodnight to Mom and Dad. We would sit on their bed and chat for a little while. Gram used to stick her head in the door and say a soft goodnight. Dad sat in a large maroon-colored chair by the front window, and Mom sat on the other side of the same window, at Dad's desk. They wore pajamas, and if the night was chilly they wore robes. Mom wore a simple blue robe; Dad's was maroon—the same color as his chair. They smoked back then, though I do not remember the room smelling all that strongly of cigarettes. There was a stronger, sweet smell of talc or perfume. They always had a nightcap before going to bed, usually a light scotch with water.

On summer nights, their window was open unless there was a heavy rain. We could hear cars passing by as we spoke, as well as the occasional soft tread or slap of someone's feet as he or she passed in front of the house. Air conditioning was not common back then, and on a hot summer's night people would take walks in the evening to cool off a bit.

I can see the scene above perfectly, almost fifty years later. With a little effort, I can hear my parents' voices and observe their younger faces. I remember the desk and the ashtray, the pens and the yellow legal pads, an old adding machine. There are a few magazines on the cream-colored radiator cover in front of the window. Mom's and Dad's slippers are under their bed. The lace curtain moves just a bit, toyed with by a light summer breeze. There are lights on in the houses across the street, partially obscured by the large trees that were and I hope still are one of the real treasures of Christopher Street. There is a single street lamp, burning bright and around which hundreds of moths swirl and swirl.

Dad sits with his leg's crossed—"man style," and Mom sits in her chair which is pulled away from the desk and facing me. Her legs are crossed, too, but "ladylike." Her hair is dark, though there are wisps of gray. She keeps it in place with bobby pins.

There are separate dressers on either side of the door. My brothers, Robert and Peter, are long asleep in a room to the left. I can almost touch and feel the things I see: Mom's silver-plated hair brush and mirror set, her jewelry, the little statue of a woman with a fine china dress, stacks of letters and coupons, a few broken rosaries. On Dad's bureau are some papers, a pair of black socks, a shoe horn, his wallet, an open pack of cigarettes, and his Zippo lighter.

They smoked non-filtered Pall Malls. Mom would always get a tiny bit of tobacco on her lip when she would take a drag on her cigarette. I can see the exact way her hand would go to her lips and gently remove the little piece.

I picture myself in that room, watching them, listening to them, saying a goodnight and kissing them and then heading on upstairs to bed. I can remember the soft cheek of my mom and the sweet smell of Pond's cold cream as I kissed her. I remember the stubble on Dad's cheek as I kissed him and the faded but still unmistakable smell of the Mennen's Skin Bracer he had splashed on his freshly shaven face that morning.

What did we speak of those many nights? I cannot recall a single conversation in detail. The words escape me, but the sensual memory is strong: the smells, the sights, the colors, the breeze, the distant sound of footsteps of a long gone night walker. The memory has lasted and seems to grow stronger with each passing year, especially since my dad died a few years ago.

It is strange, even wondrous, when you think about it! We humans are constantly trying to imagine what God is like. Is the divinity male or female, near or far, all knowing, all powerful? We Christians believe that men and women are created in the image and likeness of God. So perhaps learning about God is coextensive with learning about ourselves: how we become who we are, how we remember, and what we remember.

We think of God as some sort of grandiose finished being,

and yet our lives, if they are truly human lives at all, become so only through encounters that come scented with Mennen's Skin Bracer and Pond's Cold Cream.

God's incarnate love comes to me carried by the still warm breezes of past summer nights, nights when Mom and Dad mysteriously did the "God thing" by living their vows and letting the awesome power of their love seep into and lay claim to the ordinariness of their lives. Any one of those nights were like so much leaven, working its magic over the years, stubbornly refusing to be remembered as "inconsequential."

WORDS

There exist words arranged with such care that they enable us to actually enter the world of the one who wrote them. Even though the author's world might be long ago, it comes back to life and is shared with those who read the words.

I once read a poem printed on a poster encouraging people to read that was affixed to a subway car wall in New York City. It was a poem by a Polish-born writer, Czeslaw Milosz. The words were few, and I cannot remember their order or even the exact phrasing, though I do remember their power and the place to which they brought me as I read them. The poet wrote of a long-ago scene from his youth—a simple walk home on a winter day. He wrote of snow on a fence and a hare running across a field and an old man on the same road, visible just out of the corner of the poet's youthful eye and soon to vanish forever. It was a scene once real but long gone, but the words evoked in me the passing mystery of all things.

My heart was heavy that day. I was with my brother Johnny and we were riding the subway from a restaurant in Greenwich Village up the West Side of Manhattan. I was to leave for the Trappist monastery in a few days, and we both knew it was a parting of the ways that was qualitatively different from any previous separation we had experienced. Johnny and I had seen much of each other over the years, and this definitive change in our relationship was painful for us both. We realized that many simple and ordinary activities that we had shared over the years would no longer be possible. Johnny shared my happiness over my long-considered decision to follow the way of life at the Trappist monastery in Conyers, Georgia, far away from Manhattan—both geographically and spiritually. The pain of leaving each other was sharp and deep that day.

Johnny stood next to me on the crowded subway as I read the poem that day. We both swayed quietly on the train, aware, I am sure, of the heaviness of heart we both felt. I do not know if Johnny even read the words that day, though he must have seen them often on his many commutes.

As we rode along, memories of our many lunches together, our rides to Brooklyn to see our cousin Mae, our long chats in the car as I drove him back to his upper West Side apartment late at night imbedded themselves in my soul as surely as the scene from Poland had seared itself into the imagination of Czeslaw Milosz.

The words of the poet that day made me think of the love in which we are all immersed that makes us suffer and yet rejoice and moves some of us to write of things that happened long ago to somehow redeem those things and make them live forever.

On that day, on the corner of 57th Street and Eighth Avenue, my brother hugged me as we said good-bye to each other. He held me close to him as if he wanted to hold and remember that moment. We parted, carrying within us something new: a sense of the past born with that farewell—a past that birthed a new beginning in our lives.

There is a man who used to sing opera aloud on West 57th Street. I saw him each time I went into the city from my parish in Newark. He suffered from what might be considered a disturbed condition, but he did not seem to care what others may have thought of him as they passed him by. He just sang with all his heart, looking up at the skyscrapers all around him. He seemed quite happy to me. He probably took whatever money was offered him for his arias, though I do not recall ever having seen a little tin cup. I only remember seeing him with his hands folded on his chest, his eyes raised to the heavens as he sang.

He was there the day my brother and I parted, and I hope that he is still there today as I write this.

My words will probably never find their way onto the wall of any subway car, but they have found their way into this book. What have I to remember? No hare, no snow, no old man passing. But I have other etchings on my heart: a hug from my brother, the song of a man on a street, a ride uptown, a poem on a subway poster. These things bespeak a mystery that lives through all of us; rides with all of us; enfolds, beckons, moves, loves all of us.

THE GIFT OF WINE AND CHEESE

Mr. and Mrs. Fisher owned a store on Watchung Avenue in Montclair, New Jersey, where I grew up. It was a small store, with a soda counter, toys and candies, cigars and cigarettes, school supplies and newspapers and magazines.

The Fishers were Jewish, as I and all the kids knew because they closed the store on days that seemed odd to us. We were used to our own feasts and holidays, but we were just beginning to appreciate the other religious and cultural worlds that people inhabited, even though they lived and worked on the same streets as we did. It was, after all, the Sixties, that decade of budding tolerance for those who are somehow different from ourselves.

I can still hear the sound of the store's screen door that swung open and closed hundreds of times each summer afternoon. "Fisher's" was a favorite hangout for the kids of the neighborhood, and the couple never chased us out. Mr. Fisher was a kind man, short and always neatly dressed. He like cigars and took great pleasure in nursing a stub for hours, carefully laying it aside in the ashtray he always kept within reach. His wife was a pleasant-looking woman and a great listener. She loved to hear us talk about school and home life, and she was sympathetic (way more than most of our parents were) to the trials and tribulations of growing up in an increasingly crazy world. I do not think that I ever saw her when she was not drying a dish or a glass, or wiping the long linoleum counter and ringing out the cloth after each pass.

The Fishers had one son, who was studying to be a doctor. He worked in the store on his vacations from school, and we were in awe of his being so smart that he was going to be a doctor. I suppose that none of us had ever met a medical student before. His parents were very proud of him, of course, but looking back I imagine that many of the long hours they worked were in large measure to pay for their son's education. I can't even remember the young man's name, but I remember thinking even then that he would make a good doctor. He would be in his mid-sixties by now.

I wonder where he is these days.

A man named Walt worked at the store, too, cleaning dishes and doing odd jobs. He lived upstairs from the store. He was thin, had wispy red hair, and his fingers were yellowed from all the Pall Malls he smoked one after another. Again in retrospect, he was probably a "poor soul" that the Fisher's had befriended and took care of. I do not recall his ever mentioning family of his own. Walt lived a hermit-like existence but seemed to enjoy the parade of kids who all got to know him.

My twin brother, Jimmy, also worked at the store for the last year or so before he was killed while in high school in an automobile accident just a few blocks away from Watchung Avenue. I can still see Jimmy in his apron, taking orders and getting a kick out of learning to make different kinds of sodas and to use the cash register and make correct change. The Fishers liked him, and I was proud to have my brother working at the place where we all hung out.

I could not go into the store for weeks after Jimmy's death, because it was too painful for me.

The day I got up the courage to go back was a warm July day, about two months after the accident. I just walked in and sat at the counter. I could feel the Fishers looking at each other and then at me, and then they both came over to where I was sitting. Mr. Fisher took the cigar out of his mouth, and Mrs. Fisher put her cloth down and nervously wiped her hands on her apron. "We were afraid you would never come back," she said, "but we would have understood." Mr. Fisher looked at his wife and nodded his head in agreement. "But we are glad you are back," she continued. "How are things going at home?"

I told them what I could about so many things that had taken place in my family since and to some degree because of Jimmy's death. I said that we were all doing the best we could, but that is was very difficult. I probably started to cry, although I didn't want to.

Mr. Fisher excused himself and went into the back of the store. I heard the rear door open and close.

Mrs. Fisher told me that people had been asking after my family: Walt, Mrs. Osgoode who also lived upstairs, the Greek couple next door who owned a small delicatessen, the Neumanns who ran the bakery a few stores away, and others who lived or worked on the block. They all constituted a real, extended family, and the Behrens, in our grief, had been adopted as part of that family. They mourned my family's loss, and we were all blessed because of their mourning.

I heard the back door open again, and Mr. Fisher reappeared carrying on his arm a basket, covered with cellophane and done up with a ribbon, containing a bottle of red wine and some cheese. "For your family," he said as he awkwardly handed me the bundle, "with our condolences." He looked at me with tenderness and smiled, and then he looked around for his cigar.

I thanked them both and said that I had to get home. They asked me to come back often, and so I did. I returned to that little store throughout the years I was a seminarian and then a priest of the Archdiocese of Newark. Long after the Fishers were gone, and Walt and Mrs. Osgoode and the Greek couple and the Neumanns had either moved away or passed on, I still went back. And when I did I always remembered things old and yet ever new, things so needed wherever we human beings find ourselves—whether the streets of the old neighborhood, a newly yuppified block, a suburban housing development, the family farm, or a Trappist monastery outside of Atlanta.

We need the compassion expressed with wine and cheese, the simple gifts we give each other in times of sorrow. We need to become one extended family, where the pain of one is shared by all. We need to realize that such love is born only from suffering—which is perhaps the most profound and enduring mystery of all.

THE GIRL WHO TRIED
TO TASTE THE MOON

The pier extended quite far, and the surf of the Atlantic swayed below. The ocean was calm and, as far as one could see, it glistened and rippled.

The pier was at Seaside Heights, a popular resort area on the Jersey shore, and was called Amusement Pier because there were rides and attractions for most of its length. At the end of the pier was an area where people could stand and gaze at the beauty of the ocean and the enormous expanse of the sky. On a summer night, the pier was ablaze with a dazzling array of thousands of colored lights that rose and fell and swayed with the rides. The smells of popcorn, pizza, sausages, hot dogs, and the ocean itself blended to make an aroma that was unique.

Peals of laughter and delight filled the air and mixed effortlessly with the ceaseless sounds of the rides as they carried young and old far into the night sky. One ride, a large globe covered with small square pieces of glass, had long swings attached to it. The globe slowly turned, and those who rode the swings glided peacefully out and over the surf. It was my favorite ride, and I would some times stay on for an hour, riding in the sky high above the sea, my hands tightly holding the chains of the swing.

One evening, I walked to the end of the pier. The sky was filled with stars, and an enormous moon appeared to be rising out of the ocean. I still do not know why the moon, at particular places and times, appears to be much larger than usual. From where I stood on the pier that night, though, it looked many times its normal size. Its craters and valleys were easily discernible, and even the shadows of its mountains could be seen. It seemed so large and so near that it could be touched. Which is exactly what a small child was trying to do.

She was a little girl, seated in a stroller right near me. Her parents had come to the end of the pier, and the magic of the moon had worked its charm on them. The were kissing and holding hands as they contemplated the beauty of the moon.

They were kind of ignoring their daughter, but I observed that the little girl appeared fascinated by the rising moon, which was bathing the ocean with a generous amount of light that spread as it rose. She could not seem to take her eyes off of the enormous orb of yellow that was before her.

Suddenly, she reached out and tried to touch the moon. Then she laughed and squealed as she put her fingers to her mouth. I have no idea what she was trying to do, but it looked to me as if she were trying to take a piece of the delicious-looking moon and taste it.

We live in an age when we too readily leave to science answers to questions concerning the true nature of all things. If the ultimate meaning of life is inseparable from the deepest longings of our hearts, however, then perhaps poets and moon tasters of all ages are closer to the real answers than the Noble-laureates might be.

Perhaps there is a lesson for all of us to learn from that little girl on the boardwalk. Physicists tell us that everything that exists enjoys a relationship of reciprocity with everything else.

The tiniest bits of matter are made for each other and somehow "know" each other, even though separated by millions of miles and, in some instances, by time itself. So we humans long for the rest of creation, for the near yet at once so far, for that which exists both in and out of time. We hunger for love that never dies and for eternal life for ourselves and those we know and love. We pray that our losses be redeemed, that there is in fact a greater power who hears our prayers and knows our needs.

Is it not true that when we want to describe the truth of what lies in our hearts, we take our images from the vastness of the sea, the heights of the mountains, the fire of the stars?

Is it any wonder that we would want to taste the moon?

A DYING WOMAN'S GIFT

Every so often we have an experience that breaks through to the heart like a gush of wisdom, love, pain and strength all at once. It comes from no exact place but it illumines everything. Like an unexpected gust of wind, it cleans, reveals, sweeps away until everything seems holy.

I had such a wondrous experience one day several years ago, before I entered the monastery. It involved two meals, a moth, love, and a dying woman.

It was the day before Halloween, and I had dinner that night with friends, Jean and Carl and their three boys. I sat in their home, listening to the flow of words that summarized the events of the day and touched on the more intimate concerns that bind all families together.

From where I sat, I could see a moth outside a large patio sliding door, beating its wings against the glass, drawn to the light hanging above the kitchen table. It was an out-of-season moth, destined by fate and instinct to beat its wings futilely and alone. Seemingly, it had no other reason for its existence other than to remind me that some things have no purpose.

Before dinner, grace was said, with all of us holding hands. Young Matthew had a headache and did not feel like eating, so he excused himself and headed up to his bedroom. His twin, Daniel, complained about having to get up so early every morning to catch the school bus. He then began to make an impression of the bus driver's face, twisting his cheeks and mouth beyond all normal proportion. He seemed satisfied that he had "captured" the right contortion so as to resemble the not-well-liked bus driver, so he let go of the face and laughed at himself.

After dinner, Jean brought out a Halloween cake, decorated with orange icing and candles. Matthew had by then returned to the table, his face a bit puffy. He and Daniel blew out the candles in a pro forma way, not making any wishes. Their older brother David soon came in, not hungry and annoyed that he had to work late and that there was to be a party at his workplace the next day to which he was expected to go in costume. His brothers made fun of him and continued eating the orange colored cake. David left in a huff to go work out at the YMCA.

The moth was still at the window, now being carefully watched by a slightly higher order of created being, Fluffy the cat, who sat before the glass watching the erratic movements of the lost and tantalizing insect. The cat's head moved back and forth in tandem with the movements of the moth.

Earlier that same day, I had had lunch with Chickie and Rose, who had been friends with each other for more than thirty years. Chickie had called me earlier in the week to tell me that Rose had terminal cancer. She was afraid that Rose would not live to see Christmas. As we sat and talked at Chickie's house, Rose talked about her job, her children, and her husband. She spoke carefully about those things that meant the most to her, showing me pictures of her new granddaughter. She ate well, which surprised Chickie, but after an hour she looked at the clock and said that she had to get going.

I walked her to her car, and as she was opening the car door I told her that I knew about her illness and would be glad to talk or just be with her if she needed me. She smiled, and said that she was not afraid of dying. She took my hand and gently squeezed it, telling me some of the many things that she wanted to do before she died. That afternoon, she said, she was going Christmas shopping.

I kissed Rose on the cheek and she drove off. I stood there and waved, but she did not look back.

Going into the house, I sat with Chickie for a while. She told me that when she found out about Rose's disease, all she could say to her friend was "I love you."

I finally left Chickie's house, and headed over to Jean and Carl's, with Rose very much on my mind. She was preparing to leave "here" and was probably remembering scenes from her life just like the one I was experiencing now—quiet moments with family, all vivid to her in a new and sharply painful way.

I watched the cat and the moth. I saw an upset older son and heard the laughter of younger brothers. I listened to the day's worries. As the family rounded off the closing moments of another day of their lives together, I thought of Rose, gathering gifts as we ate, moving from aisle to aisle in a nearby mall, determined to leave behind gifts chosen and wrapped with love.

As I connected her and what was transpiring before me, it was if the room were spun from pure gold. The words of the family were sheer loveliness. The laughter of the boys echoed the grace of the entire universe. The kitchen light glowed like a jewel, and the cat and the moth seemed to be engaged in something of eternal significance.

The memory of that day and those two meals—so close together and somehow connected—has incredible power for me.

I do not know the gifts Rose bought for others that night,

but this memory is mine: I will always have the image of her, driven to buy and wrap one more present for each of those she loved.

"I love you."

Those words do more than fill the air. They carry the very meaning of the life that is God's. They whisper once, three times, a million times, that nothing is in vain—not the beating of the wings of a moth against a pane of cold glass, nor the blowing out of candles on a bright orange cake, nor the careful selection of gifts by a dying woman.

THE PRESENCE OF GOD

Father Pat was born and raised in Tanzania. I met him only once, quite a few years ago when he came to raise money for the missions at the parish where I was an associate pastor. I connected with him right away, because we both liked to talk about philosophy, religion, and the separate worlds we inhabited.

As we sat in the rectory living room and spoke that evening, we could hear boys playing touch football in our church parking lot. They used to play there almost every summer night, and I used to sit on the front steps of the rectory and watch them. That night they had a special appeal to me in light of what Pat and I were discussing. We spoke of essences and ways of arriving at them, using the exotic language of philosophy. But what we were getting at was happiness and love and the existence of God, and it occurred to me that the kids already had all that figured out instinctively.

Pat had been raised in a village in Africa. His people did not have libraries, computers, televisions, and the like. Youngsters were taught by their elders what was deemed important, and they would all chant together until the presence of God was very real to them. Pat said that the children simply *knew* that God was present. Then he laughed and corrected himself. No, he said, it wasn't a *knowing* as much as it was a *feeling*.

It struck me that night, and it continues to strike me as I remember it from behind the monastery walls, how differently Pat and his people experienced God from most of us in the West. Is it possible that because of our lingering insistence on tracking God with the radar of our minds that we refuse to venture a trusting yet uncertain journey toward God with our hearts, our feelings, our intuition? Wouldn't it be a wondrous thing if we could experience everything as grace, believe that there is nothing that is not of God, accept every day as an invitation to leave the shelter of our minds and see, touch and rejoice in divine life?

The boys playing football in a parking lot in Newark and the young people chanting with their elders in Tanzania already experienced the presence of God—whether they could articulate it or not. Religion should not concern itself with what is "in" or "out," what is "sacred" or not. It should not become a frame that holds us but rather helps us burst through all frames. It should be inclusive, hopeful, not afraid of looking in the wrong places. True religiosity has a self-correctiveness to it that leaves plenty of room for art, poetry, dance, chanting, and playing a game of ball on a hot summer's night.

Ours is an age and a society that seeks God more than ever. Our minds are understandably weary from the overload of thought that seems to have exhausted itself and does not know how to be refreshed. But God is present despite our effort or lack of effort, despite our awareness or our lack of awareness.

THE FACE OF PAIN

His name I cannot remember, though his face is as vivid to me as it was when I last saw him almost fifteen years ago. He was nine years old and used to come to early Mass with his mother almost every morning at a parish in Newark where I was an associate pastor for many years. They sat in the first pew, and I soon realized that she was coaching him in the routines for being an altar server.

The day finally came for the meeting of new servers, and his mother dropped the boy off before any of the other kids arrived. She told me that he was eager to serve Mass but was worried that he might not get along with the others. I asked her why, and she said that he was a loner. I noticed later at the practices that he did keep his distance, but he proved to be trustworthy and polite. In fact, he had an eagerness to please that broke my heart, for I sensed that he was hurting very much in his young life.

I asked the pastor about the boy and he told me that there were serious marriage problems in the home. He did not elaborate, but I then understood the boy's sadness and need for acceptance.

Several weeks ago, while I was praying before the Blessed Sacrament, I thought about the boy again. His face simply "arrived" in my mind's eye, even though I could not think of anything that would have triggered it. Perhaps I was praying for all the people in pain in the world, and the boy's face simply embodies that suffering for me.

I thought back to those first months after I met him. He looked undernourished and sad even when he smiled. It was the kind of smile that pleads for help and recognition. He did fine as an altar boy, and then for some reason stopped coming. I never saw him again. The pastor said that the family had moved away, and I remember thinking that there must have been financial problems that forced them to relocate.

Ever since that time, that little boy's face has been to me a window or a mirror through which I observed something that exists in each of us. It is said that human pain is an invariant, that is, it is one of the few constants that all people of all cultures experience. To be human is, at least partially, to suffer pain. But pain is not only something that happens to us from the outside. At its most fundamental level, it is an ongoing part of the human condition and it comes from within. Yet we are constantly hit from all sides—in the media, in the taken-for-granted ethos of our times—with the idea that pain is abnormal, unusual, unacceptable. We are made to believe that when and where pain exists, it can simply be eradicated by taking the right medication, finding the right therapist or support group, thinking the right way, reading the right book, moving to the right place.

That little boy's face speaks volumes to me. In it I see the hurt in all of us, the hurt that comes from our estrangement from God and from each other. It is a hurt that is not going to go away, but it is one that we can make more tolerable for one another if we really try.

A "GRACE UNKNOWN"

Many years ago, I visited Lourdes, France, the site of the appearances by Our Lady to a young girl named Bernadette. I was then in my early twenties, but some scenes from the visit are still quite vivid in my mind's eye. I remember a rainy afternoon and a woman selling beautiful flowers from a cart. She was dressed in a plastic rain coat and sat beneath a large umbrella. I took a photograph of her, and was impressed later with how the streets glistened in the finished black and white print.

I recall the large crowds and being particularly impressed by the candlelight procession that was held each evening. A line of pilgrims stretched for what seemed miles, and their flickering candles could be seen far into the distance—a long, magic road of soft light that moved with majesty and reverence towards the shrine.

The shrine itself was simple: a statue of Mary, made of a pure white material, nestled in a grotto. Water ran nearby, believed to carry with it the favors and blessings of the Mother of God. Vigil lights burned in blue and red glass, lit in hope for miracles yet to come and in gratitude for those already granted. A sense of the miraculous permeated the air. On the walls of the grotto were hung many hundreds of canes, crutches, braces, and other joyously discarded helps for those once disabled and now cured. At any given time during our visit there, the disabled and ill could be readily seen throughout the crowds.

I confess that back then I did not give much thought to the miraculous. If asked what I thought about it all, I probably would have responded that I wanted proof, to see and experience for myself—on my own terms—what seemingly defied rational explanation. Although I was not able to explain all the discarded crutches and the like, I was also aware that not all who made the trip to Lourdes were cured. Perhaps I wanted to believe but did not know how. Or, perhaps the circumstances of my life then did not warrant a need to believe. I was young, my life was good; my desperate and hurting straits were still far down the road. You might say that I was skeptical, but in fact I was quite self-contained. Nothing outside of what I could provide from my own resources seemed necessary or even desirable. I was, in short, religiously smug.

On Sunday, my companions and I attended Mass in the large and beautiful shrine. The homily was by a priest who spoke French, and I knew enough French back then to follow what he was saying. He was an older man, and he spoke with gentleness. He said that he knew that many in the church had come to Lourdes with specific requests for a miracle, which he felt was well and good. But he went on to develop his thoughts about grace *inconnu* or "unknown." Although we may not receive what we specifically ask, he insisted, much more than what we request is indeed given, no one is ever deprived of grace, and grace arrives "unknown" in wondrously unexpected ways.

This old priest seemed to want desperately to share a sense that life is an unending shower of blessings. As I write this memory, I somehow associate his words with my father's death in a small hospital in Louisiana, not far from the monastery.

Dad had been ill for some time, and we knew that his life was nearing an end. He knew that, too. His wife and his sons and daughters, knowing in our hearts that he was suffering and would die, prayed for many miracles. The most obvious one—that would Dad get better, leave the hospital, return home again, and resume his former life—seemed beyond hope. Yet we wanted something good and tangible to come from the terrible pain he was experiencing and from the sorrow of losing him from our lives. We prayed for grace, but it was a "grace unknown."

Dad did die, and it was a beautiful death. His family shed many tears of grief, but we did experience a small miracle in the many good and loving people—family, friends, doctors, nurses, ministers and others—who visited him and gave him whatever love and care they had to give. They formed a long, magic road of soft light that moved with majesty and reverence through his hospital room. They provided my father with all he really needed to die in peace.

They were "grace unknown"—words from a sermon I heard many years ago and only now understand.

GOD IN THE DETAILS

When I was first entering the monastery, I shared with a friend of mine that I was afraid that my friendships back home would be lost or at least frozen in time, that I would not know how to keep them alive and a vital part of me.

My friend smiled at me and said that all those I love would go with me and grow in my heart in new and deeper ways. "Just continue to love all of us," she said, "and God will take care of the details." I think I have learned what she meant from my friends Jimmy and Mary.

Jimmy and Mary own a farm in northern New Jersey. I served in a parish there for several years shortly after I was ordained. That was over twenty-five years ago, and I have gone to their home for dinner often over the years. Jimmy is a big man with a ready smile who cannot do enough for you. Mary is sweet and bright and giving. After dinner, we would go to their living room and sit and talk for hours. The room was large and comfortable, with all sorts of unique things from their travels and antique shows. There was a large tropical fish tank in the corner, which bubbled away as we chatted. Through a large window that faced the back yard I could see the trees and the fences where they kept exotic animals they raised for zoos: horses, ostriches, emus, goats, miniature deer. On many a warm summer night, Jimmy would walk me around the farm and show me the newer additions. He was always proud of the animals and delighted in showing them off to me.

When I first started to write, I would type up my essays

(this was before the advent of word processing and e-mail) and bring them with me when I went to their home. They would put them aside, and by the next time I visited they would have read them and told me how they liked them. One night, Jimmy seemed especially animated when we sat down after dinner. "I have to tell you something," he said. "The piece you wrote about Pine Street is the best ever."

I had given them an essay the week before about one of the streets in the town near them. "It's the details," Jimmy proclaimed. "I could picture everything: the Chinese restaurant with the little Buddha statue and candle; the kids playing in the street; the liquor store on the corner; the lady on the porch across the street. Know what? Mary and I just had to look at the street again. We actually drove into town, and it's all there, just like you said."

Jimmy was right. I did embellish that essay with a lot of details, and I could remember hesitating to do so while I was writing it. I wanted to make a point, I remember, and did not want to have the details get in the way. Yet here was Jimmy, enthralled more with the details than with whatever point I was trying to make, enthusiastic enough to hop in a van and drive twelve miles to check them out, as he said, "for real."

Jimmy writes me frequently. His penmanship is beautiful and he always uses fine onion-skin paper. I love his letters and have told him so.

They are filled with details—about his wife, his sons and grandchildren, his exotic animals. I can experience them right on the page, almost as if I were still walking around the farm.

But I am here in my room, and it is getting late. The monastic day starts early, so I will go to bed soon.

I will write Jimmy and Mary tomorrow morning, long before the sun rises over both Georgia and New Jersey. I know now that our friendship will last our lifetimes and will develop and grow...as long as we all pay attention to the details.

THE PARADE

I like the sense of proportion and perspective that thrives in the small town of Madisonville, Louisiana, where my parents moved after they retired. The conversations that go on in the barber shop or beauty parlor bring global things down to manageable proportions. The old library is roughly the size of the average drive-in bank but is well used—even more so than the new large library that is some distance from the town.

One of my visits home from the monastery coincided with Mardi Gras. My parents asked me if I wanted to go with them that afternoon to the parade. I declined at first, thinking that they wanted to drive to New Orleans for one of the grand-scale parades there. But Mom said that the parade was right in Madisonville, so we all walked down to see it.

It was indeed to be a small parade, on a small street in a small town, with low tech and few expectations. The floats were lined up at the end of the tree lined main avenue, waiting to begin their slow, brief journey into the spotlight.

People watched from the porches of homes, welcoming friends and strangers alike to stop for something to drink and eat. Finally, the signal was given and the parade began. There were quite a few people lining the street, sitting on lawn chairs and clapping and cheering as the floats approached. It seemed that every organization in town was represented on one float or another, and I noticed that there was a great degree of reciprocal recognition shared between those on the floats and those on the streets. Everybody, in short, knew and liked one other, at least for that afternoon, and a genuine sense of neighborliness filled the March air.

The king and queen of the parade sat on the most brightly colored float, tossing shiny coins into the air in the direction of people who approached as the float glided by. The setting sun was a perfect backdrop to this small and colorful drama that unfolded on each block.

When they reached us, my mother raised her hands and caught three coins. Children scrambled around her, laughing and snatching coins from the air and off the street. Some of the children, however, were too small or too slow and were not able to catch any of the coins. Mom noticed their plight and, with great maternal pleasure, gave her coins to the disappointed children nearest her.

I watched the float pass into the golden sun and thought of the great parade of life. In our younger seasons, we raise our hearts and hands, hoping to catch whatever love may come our way. But with age and wisdom—and after more than a few parades—we learn to find delight in giving our love away, becoming all the richer for it.

BROTHER LIFE, SISTER DEATH

About twenty years ago, I used to bring the Eucharist to a woman named Katrina. She was in her late fifties and was dying at home from lung cancer. I remember her room as if I had been there yesterday. She collected antique lamps, and they warmed the room with a soft yellow light. I still think of her every time I see a Tiffany lamp or a kerosene lantern.

But it was Katrina who was the true light in that room.

She was not in a lot of pain, but she knew that she was dying. The smell of death was in the room. Whatever antiseptics were used could not fully conceal the smell of her disease. She was embarrassed by it and used to cover her mouth as she spoke to me, but I did not mind the odor.

She had remarkable faith and said things to me that I did not understand then. She had gone through whatever treatments were available and was weary and further weakened from them. She was not "resigned" to her approaching death, yet she was not bitter either. She welcomed death as a benevolent stranger—an unknown person she wanted to befriend, even though she knew it would take her life.

I found something of God in Katrina. God spoke to me through her suffering, her loving, her hoping and her dying.

One morning, she asked me to hold her hand and pray with her. She gently clasped my hand and squeezed it just a bit, closing her eyes and smiling. We prayed, or rather she prayed. (I did not know what prayer really was back then.) She whispered prayers of love and hope for her children and her husband, and prayed to make the most of what little time she had left.

Then she looked down at her wasted body and addressed the cancer that had darkened and eaten away her lungs. "Strange friend," she said, "my disease that eats so close to my heart, I am at peace with you. *You* will bring me to God."

She comforted herself with her uncanny faith and confidence, transforming her disease from an enemy to a friend. She whispered softly to it and embraced its untimeliness.

Katrina certainly would not have been hostile to a cure. She loved life and would have welcomed more of it. She cried many times at the thought of not being able to touch, speak or simply be with her family. But she trusted God completely and allowed her weakness to become her strength.

Looking back, I marvel at what a gift Katrina was to me, a young priest just beginning to grasp the implications of our faith. I was there with her family, holding her hand when she died, and I knew in the depths of my being that at the moment of death she did not cease to exist but became something more.

"Brother life, sister death," she used to call them. "The secret is learning to love both, Father," she told me.

MEMORIES OF GRACE

A friend of mine stopped by the monastery recently, relating an experience that jolted him from his workaday routine. He was trying to fix a bug in his computer and was exasperated. Sitting back in his chair, he fixed his eyes on the whirling ceiling fan directly above him. Its blades turned slowly in a wide circling motion, and my friend was captivated by them for several moments. He said he had a sense of profound peace while watching the fan and felt the experience prompting him to remember a specific image or truth that he knew but had forgotten. It was, he said, as if God was trying to tell him something. The turning blades triggered an association he could not quite grasp or bring sharply into focus, but he knew that it was important.

The meaning of the experience became more and more elusive the more he tried to seize it through the manipulations of his conscious mind. Yet days later he remained fascinated by the intrusion of the lazily turning blades into his consciousness.

I have had similar experiences, and I also do not know what they mean. One is a time when I was a parish priest in Newark. It was six in the morning on a cold winter day. There was no visible rising of the sun because it was snowing heavily. I saw an old woman, all bundled up, shuffling heavily through the as yet unplowed church parking lot on her way to early Mass. As she passed beneath a streetlight, I saw thousands of snow flakes swirl and spin madly around her before coming to rest on the ground. Suddenly, she stopped before a statue of the Blessed

Mother, bowed her head, placed her hand to her lips, and then touched the base of the statue. After a moment, she walked on—out of the light and toward the church door.

And that's it! I don't know who the woman was, I don't know what the memory means, I don't know why it has such a hold on me. But there it is—just like my friend's twirling fan—going round and round in my mind, evoking an insight that remains just out of reach, pointing to some deep truth I know but cannot articulate.

Here's another memory. I was ten or eleven years old and sitting in church one Sunday. I had a runny nose and kept sniffling. I was too old, I must have thought then, to wipe my nose on my sleeve yet too young to leave the pew and go looking for a tissue on my own. A lady with red hair tapped me on the shoulder from the pew behind me and handed me a wad of fresh tissues. I remember clearly, even to this day, how relieved I was.

There are no other memories from the hundreds of Masses I attended as a youth that stand out as sharply as this one does. I cannot call to mind, for example, an image of one priest saying Mass, but I remember that lady and can still see her face in my mind's eye. I think that I would recognize her immediately were I to see her again after all these years.

These vague memories are somehow a window to our souls. They disclose things to us, even prior to our consciousness or interpretation of them. Bidden or not bidden, the image of the old woman, walking against the cold wind, determined to go to Mass on a dark, harsh winter morning, comes to me. My friend, mesmerized by a fan, watches the blades turn and turn, feeling his heart move toward something he knows but cannot quite put his finger on. I remember a red-haired lady's single act of kindness to me and yet cannot recall anything else of that day or so many other days. It is as if some memories have a life and intent of their own. They seem to have their own reasons for coming, for staying, for leaving, even for hiding their meaning from our hearts and minds.

Yet how beautiful that old woman, gently kissing the Madonna in the swirling snow. How vibrant the lady's red hair as she handed me the salvific tissue. How hypnotic that ceiling fan. Might they all be calling us to a deeper reality, a divine presence? Might they be memories of grace?

Therefore I intend to keep on reminding you of these things, though you know them already and are established in the truth that has come to you.

—2 PETER 1:13

A CIRCUS OF SURPRISES

When I lived near New York City, I used to go to Washington Square, a small park in the heart of Greenwich Village. On a summer's day, if I was lucky enough to find a place to sit on one of the parks benches, I would stay for hours, people watching. It was a circus of surprises.

There was a man who walked around on stilts, with make-up on his face and a Mohawk haircut.

Numerous jugglers threw their colored balls and pins into the air before delighted crowds of people. Old men sat at tables playing chess, checkers and other games. Some of them had their dogs with them, who seemed to enjoy the human spectacle parading before their eyes as much as I did.

Vendors galore sold their goods on the fringes of the park. Soda, popcorn, hot dogs and chestnuts were the usual fare. Just outside the park, others had watches, jewelry, incense and books for sale, spread out on rugs on the sidewalk.

There were fortune tellers who plied their talent from tables placed underneath the trees. The area had a real carnival atmosphere to it.

I remember one guy who had set up a little podium and was warning his listeners about the imminent coming of the last days. Well versed in the symbolism of the Apocalypse, he hammered at his small audience with ways and means of saving their souls before the fiery end. I was pleased to note that the man placed a box in front of the podium, hoping for donations. He must not have thought that the end was all that near!

I marveled at a guy on a unicycle who seemed to find exquisite delight in weaving his way through the crowded sidewalks. He was young, had earrings, and sported colorful running shorts and a tie-dyed tight-fitting shirt.

There were musicians who played flutes, guitars, violins, drums, and countless other instruments, their empty music cases opened at their feet, hoping that onlookers would toss in a few coins.

Artists created picturesque scenes right on the sidewalks of the park, using chalks and pastels. It amazed me that they would put so much effort into their work, knowing that its beauty would be washed away with the next rain or dirtied by the feet of those who would soon walk over it.

There were few restraints on human expression in the park. Lovers kissed and caressed freely—women kissing men, men kissing women, men kissing men, women kissing women. Young children of all colors and nationalities played together. The square was a kaleidoscope of tastes and cultures. Each slight turn of my head offered another fascinating scene. I used to wonder what I was missing elsewhere in the park if I kept my attention riveted too long in one place.

I suppose that I looked very conventional, sitting there on my bench. I actually envied those who dared to dress or act wildly, who would spend hours creating beauty for free, knowing that it would soon vanish.

Now that I look back from my current venue behind cloistered walls, what appealed most to me about Washington Square was the element of surprise. It seems to me that the church of all places should be a circus of surprises—not necessarily the kind

I found in Washington Square but rather the kind that encourages us to take risks, to resist the predictable and the taken-for-granted, to lovingly support one another when we take roads that turn out to be dead ends.

After all, we are the followers of the biggest surprise of all: the God who actually became a human being and was born—surprise of surprises—of what was the ultimate in lowly, obscure and unlikely origins. We believe that by this act God has turned all of creation into one, big, slowly unwrapping gift box, bearing within it things "eyes have not seen and ears have not heard."

We Christians should act as if life were one big Washington Square. That is the good news the church has to offer.

THE ROSE

A long time ago, when I was a young parish priest, I raised roses. One day, a woman friend of mine asked if she could have a particular rose that stood out in the garden from all the rest. So I went into the rectory and found a scissors and carefully cut a beautiful salmon colored rose from the bush, taking care to cut a long stem. I gave the rose to my friend and she placed it next to her cheek to feel the softness of its petals. She smelled it and smiled at its fragrant loveliness.

It was, I thought to myself, a near perfect rose. Yet there were others—faded whites and reds and creams—that were wilted and sagging, dying beyond their usefulness. We both ignored them, but I remember wondering later if anyone had stood before them and admired their beauty before it had been lost.

My friend took the rose home and placed it in the best vase she owned, a Waterford. She placed a penny and an aspirin in the water to keep the rose fresh, for they supposedly would do something to the water to stall, for a while, the decay of the rose. I remember stopping by her house a few days later, and the rose indeed still looked fresh and beautiful.

Not long ago, I left the monastery for a day and went to a nearby shopping mall with another monk. The mall was crowded and we walked down the large, wide aisles, gazing at the shoppers and looking into the store windows. The stores were filled with things comedian Billy Crystal might describe as "marvelous." There were jewels and furs and leathers, designer clothes and costly fragrances, sporting goods, silverware, gold and platinum rings, all laid out in one window after another beneath soft and alluring lights. Music played as we walked, softly accenting the atmosphere as we moved from one shop window to the next. We were hungry and stopped at the large food court for something to eat. Even there, fullness abounded. There were many cultural delicacies in a variety of different booths.

After lunch, I sat in the mall and grew quiet, for amidst all that abundance there was nothing I really wished to buy (even if I had any money, which I didn't). For some reason, I recalled the salmon-colored rose. The mall seemed to me like a garden, filled with people of all kinds of aspirations, accomplishments and failures. I found that my eyes and thoughts were attracted to some and not to others. Like my friend with the rose, I deemed some more worthy of being noticed than others.

Many mystics have long testified to the existence of a higher state of consciousness—an experience of being one with all that is.

But most of us usually see this dimly at best.

As one rose is eyed for its beauty, the others fade from site. Likewise, as we differentiate among people, we lose sight of what is good and common among all people.

From now on, I'm not going to cut any roses. They are all part of the same bush, the same beauty, the same existence.

WALKER PERCY
AND THE AMERICAN EXPRESS CARD

People often ask me why I started writing at a relatively late age. (I was in my forties when I first started sending out articles for publication.) I have one person to thank, and this little memory of grace is about him.

The Kumquat is a bookstore in Covington, Louisiana. I have gone there every time I visited my parents since they retired many years ago. It is owned by author Walker Percy's daughter, and if you go there on any Tuesday, you may be fortunate enough to meet Walker's wife, Bunt Percy. She will gladly show you the well-stacked shelves and in particular the collection of her late husband's novels and essays, displayed prominently to the left as soon as you walk in the door. Bunt has a weakness for good conversation and good soup, and there is an eatery right next door to the bookstore. So we have had many happy meals together.

Over ten years ago, when I was still a parish priest in Newark and trying to decide what to do with the rest of my life, I was in graduate school, trying to come up with a dissertation topic for a Ph.D. in literature. I had reached the point beyond exasperation and despair; there is no name for the frustration I was experiencing.

I was staying with my parents in Covington and knew that Walker Percy, the acclaimed southern novelist, lived just a few miles away. I had already read several dissertations on his writings and found them intriguing. Perhaps, I thought, I could add something to the body of knowledge about this great Catholic American author.

I had heard about the Kumquat and went in one day and bought plenty of books by and about Walker Percy. The bill came to well over $150.00, and I was glad that I had my American Express card. I purchased the books with the card, and when the lady at the cash register asked for my telephone number I gave my parents' number.

I remember going home with my books in a yellow plastic bag and refusing to tell my dad how much they cost. I mumbled something to him about their being very modestly priced, but little did I know what a bargain they were.

That afternoon, I sat and read through some of the essays in *Lost in the Cosmos*, a collection of satirical essays by Walker Percy. My mom called me out of my reverie when it was time for dinner, and during the course of the meal I told my parents how excited I was about Percy's writings. I thought that I could soon come up with a workable topic on him for my dissertation.

Shortly after dinner, the telephone rang and Mom answered it.

When my mother gets excited, she blushes a bit and her voice rises a little bit above its norm. I could tell that the telephone call was something out of the ordinary.

It was Walker Percy himself on the line. He wanted to speak to "the man who had bought so many books."

I will never forget how nervous I was when Mom handed me the receiver. I took the phone and introduced myself. I told him that I was a priest, loved his writings, and was desperately in need of a dissertation topic.

He invited me to his home for lunch the next day.

I lay awake long into the night with anticipation. In the morning I actually went and got a haircut. Since I did not bring any good shoes on my visit, Dad let me borrow his. I also wore one of his best shirts.

I carefully followed the directions that the writer had given me, particularly keeping in mind his warning to watch out for their big Doberman. Walker Percy greeted me as I pulled in front of the house and we went inside. He introduced me to his dog, and together we put the pooch at ease.

Walker (he insisted that I call him that) and I sat in the back room of their house, a large sun-filled room with a window overlooking the Bogue Folaya, and chatted over drinks and lunch for several hours. We spoke of the Church, the priesthood, American and Southern culture, and especially about writing.

I told Walker that I had always wanted to write but that something held me back. That was early in the conversation, but as he walked me to my car several hours later he must have remembered what I said, because he told me that I should write what I feel and—more importantly—that I should always write with hope. He said that because I am a Christian and a Catholic priest I am "stuck with a wondrous message" and had little choice but to write about it.

This was to be the first of several times that we met over the next few years.

We also exchanged letters that are among the few possessions I kept after I entered the monastery. I remember when

I had my very first article published in 1989. It was in the *National Catholic Reporter*, which has since published many of my essays, and was about the holiness and hope I observed in a group of people who worked at Andy's Diner in Newark. Walker wrote back a warm letter of congratulations. (It is interesting that an editor from ACTA Publications also saw that article and included it in a book of readings on the spirituality of work. Over ten years later, that same editor published my first book, *Grace Is Everywhere*. So a large part of my writing career can be traced back to the encouragement of Walker Percy.)

In late 1990, Walker's letters stopped. My mom told me that she had heard that he was quite ill and that it did not look good. He died in the spring of 1991.

I wrote to his wife, Bunt, and later attended a memorial service for him that was held at Saint Ignatius Church in Manhattan. I sat in the back of the packed church and did not get a chance to speak with Bunt that day, but when I went to visit my parents shortly after Christmas that year I called her to express my condolences. She asked me to come over to the house for lunch, and we watched a football game together and chatted about a lot of things, including how much her husband had influenced my life.

She told me that she wanted to show me something, and taking me by the hand she took me into Walker's study.

She said that the room was just as he had left it when he died. She smiled and pointed to what looked like a music stand near Walker's desk. There on the stand was an article that I had sent him about my brother's death. I was stunned to see it and yet very proud. He had written a few notes in the margins, but I did not want to disturb anything, so I did not pick up the paper to read what he had written. To this day I do not know what he said, but it is not important. What is important is that such a great man would spend even a few moments reading and commenting on something a fledgling author wrote.

I gave up my American Express card when I entered the monastery, but I am glad that I once used it to buy some books. I never did come up with a dissertation topic, never did get that doctoral degree. But Walker Percy encouraged me to write with hope about what I feel, and that is what I have always tried to do. What I received from him was what I truly needed, and that's why I call it "grace."

THE STAINED-GLASS SLIPPERS

It is an image that comes from a magazine I read many years ago. What first caught my eye was the picture that accompanied the article. It was a photograph of ballerina slippers— old, worn, frayed at the toes. The once shiny satin was torn and dirty.

The story was written by the woman who had kept the slippers from her childhood, holding on to them for these many years. It seems that as a little girl her heart's desire had been to dance. In the magazine, she recalled imagining herself on a great stage, dancing ballet. In those dreams, she saw herself dancing beautifully and gracefully, seemingly without effort. She envisioned the woman she so desired to become—dancing as if floating on air, affording magical delight to thousands.

When the little girl was old enough, her mother had bought her first slippers, the ones in the photograph. Then began years of hard practice. As the woman of her dreams danced and swirled in her dreams, the real little girl of flesh and blood stumbled and fell. She ached with sore feet, torn ligaments, and many bruises, all accompanied by prolonged periods of disappointment and heartache as progress was slow and unrewarding. Still the little girl picked herself up time after time with her mother's support and encouragement. There would be many more sets of slippers, but the first she kept.

As the years passed, the falls became far less frequent. The young woman mastered the art of movement and began to dance with grace and power. She and the lovely woman of her dreams became one and the same. Now grown to adulthood, the woman keeps the old slippers as a reminder that what is truly loved and dreamed for is indeed possible—but only with effort, determination and loving support.

I look at the beautiful church at our monastery and think of the countless long-forgotten people who gave from what little they had that there might be stained glass windows, marble altars, and many things of loveliness and beauty here.

What is not reflected in the bricks and mortar, however, are their dreams—dreams that were realized through sacrifice and hard work. These are the sacrifices that make the church real and breathing and reflective of God.

I would like to raise one more stained glass window high in our church. In the center of that window would be a pair of worn-out ballerina slippers.

JOE

Early Christmas Eve many years back, I was looking out the front window of the rectory and noticed a man sprawled across the front steps of the church.

I recognized Joe, a young man suffering from alcoholism. His disease was far advanced and I am quite sure that his young age was the only thing that had staved off death.

Joe was in his early thirties. He was homeless and had gone through detox at a nearby hospital several times. He stopped by the rectory frequently for food, a cigarette, a cup of coffee, or a few dollars. He slept anywhere he could find shelter, which was usually beneath a nearby railroad trestle or in a large heated doorway in the front of a large shopping mall several blocks away from the church.

The memory of him lying there that night sticks in my mind. His isolation and despair was in such contrast to the full and expectant gatherings that would soon be taking place that night in homes and places of worship all over the world. It seemed that everyone that night, except Joe, was involved in the redemptive process.

I knew from experience that there was nothing at all we could do for Joe. Hank, our deacon, brought him inside and gave him some hot chocolate and a sandwich. We encouraged him to go to a nearby Salvation Army shelter, but Joe shook his head and headed back out into the night.

I thought how God lived in Joe, how God suffered in him, how God felt the cold concrete on his face and the sting of cold urine on his legs. The helplessness and hopelessness of any human life cannot be estranged from the reality of the God who loves every one of us, no matter what our situation or state in life. In the ever-so-human condition of Joe, God lived and waited as well, curled beneath a railroad trestle, within hearing distance of Yuletide carols and alleluias.

We Christians believe redemption—that blessed recovery of all things holy—to be an ongoing and mysterious process. We know that we shall all be redeemed in God's time and through God's love. It is something we all await. Joe will be saved, as will all who have been hurt or broken and seemingly put out of the human family.

I once tried to understand salvation as a singular, somehow approachable event—something that could be described with words between the cover of a fine text. I have come to accept it as being many seeds of living potential strewn throughout the universe, born and matured by the winds of mystery and providence. These seeds blossom only through the struggles of existence, in which the cross of Christ stands as the promise of eternal life.

This is our only hope. It is a hope that prompts a recognition of the Joe that is within us all—a helplessness in need of a cup of coffee, a place of warmth and understanding, and the healing love of God.

Watching Hank feed Joe that night, I thought of the God who feeds all of us and yet still needs to be dried and fed and clothed and sheltered.

THE LADY ON THE BUS

The #66 DeCamp is the bus I used to take from the Port Authority Bus Terminal in Manhattan back home to Montclair, New Jersey, when I was a parish priest there. I would go to Manhattan to see my brother John and then walk from his office on West 57th Street to the terminal on West 41st Street.

One night several years ago, I took the late bus and found a seat right in the front. I was glad because I liked looking out the large front window, watching the road glide smoothly beneath the bus.

A young woman was on my right. She had the window seat. She was young and pretty and could have been so many things—a business executive, a secretary, a sales clerk. There was no way to know. She was nicely dressed and, like so many women who commute back and forth to Manhattan, she wore sneakers and kept her good shoes in a bag or had left them at her workplace.

The bus pulled out into the night and wound its way down a long ramp and on through the Lincoln Tunnel. There was not much traffic at that time of night and the bus moved easily along its route. I stared straight ahead, watching all that was before me, gazing at very familiar lights and buildings along Route 3. I was absorbed in whatever was on my mind for those few miles.

Suddenly I felt a light something on my shoulder. The woman had dozed off and her head had come to rest on me. I felt a flush of panic lest she wake up and think me "forward" or worse. But I relaxed as best I could because I liked her being there and, frankly, it had been a long time since any woman had been that close to me—in a sleepily warm way, at least.

The bus rolled along the New Jersey highway. The intimate nearness of the woman made me think. I could smell the sweet fragrance of her hair. I wonder what she did for a living that made her so tired. Or maybe she had just let go the cares of the day.

And so it was that we rode for miles. I began to wonder what it would be like, sharing my life with a woman. There was nothing at all "religious" about what I was thinking, at least in a formal sense, but I experienced for those few miles the sense of a shared comfort and vulnerability that can exist between two people—a sacred and inviolable space, where it is easy and natural to trust someone enough to fall asleep on his or her shoulder.

The bus took the sharp turn off Route 3 and wound its way onto Grove Street. The swaying of the bus wakened her. She looked up at me and said "Sorry" and smiled. I said it was okay and smiled back at her. We rode on in silence to Montclair. She soon reached up and pressed the stop button a few stops before mine. She gathered her things from the bin above, and I leaned back as she left her seat and climbed off the bus. I watched her as the bus pulled away and she departed to wherever she lived— perhaps to her husband and children.

As I sit and write these words, the memory of her makes me smile to myself in this quiet, celibate monastery. We speak of love here a lot, and much of our conversation has to do with learning love's ways as God would have us know them. In a culture that easily reduces love to something akin to a possession, a right, a path of self-fulfillment that approaches self-gratification, it is hard to take seriously the kind of love that calls one out of oneself for the sake of others. But that is exactly what the monastic vocation is about—just as it is the basis for every good marriage and family.

What warms me about the memory of that bus ride was seeing the woman find a "place" of peace and trust on my shoulder, a place where thought and worry stopped, when the ride was smooth and she could let go of her busy day and sleep in peace.

THE CLEANING LADIES

There was a time I worked on Wall Street in New York, and I should not make a big deal out of it because it was not a very long period in my life. But it was a very rich one, even though I did not make a lot of money. I saw a lot, absorbed a lot, wondered a lot.

One night I worked late and was tired. It was a very cold night, and I walked from Pine and Water Streets across the tip of Manhattan to a park near the World Trade Center. I bought a cup of coffee, found an empty iron bench, and sat down. Around me were works of art: life-sized statues of commuters—both men and women—looking very real in the shadows of night. These statues were already familiar to me. There is even one of a man just like me sitting on a bench just like mine. It was as if I had become frozen there in time.

I sipped the hot coffee and looked about. The Trade Center towers rose magnificently above me, some of their lights still on. In the distance the Hudson River flowed into New York harbor, and the lights of many large ships twinkled. I could see New Jersey's lights, too. All around me the shops were closed. Only the restaurants and bars were still open. The rush hour was long over and there were few people passing by.

Suddenly, large crowds of people filled the square. Mostly women, they came to Manhattan at night to clean the offices in the buildings. I'd guess there are tens of thousands of them in Manhattan any given night. The ones I saw that night came out of the subways, where they had arrived from the Bronx, Brooklyn, Queens, New Jersey, and other parts of the metropolitan area. They carried bags and parcels and traveled in pairs, moving quickly through the city streets, anxious to get to the warmth of their workplaces and out of the bitter cold.

These women were struggling to make a better life for themselves and their families, and money was needed for that. I feel intrusive even now wondering about their lives, but I was captivated by them and believe they have something to teach all of us about the meaning of life and love and work and wealth.

I am now in a Trappist cloister in Georgia, and tonight in Manhattan I am sure the cleaning women are just arriving. They walk beneath towering signs of power and wealth and among frozen statues of business men and women. They may look around them in awe, but they have work to do, lives to live, children to feed, things to attend to. That is the way it has always been; that is the way it always will be.

I close my eyes and pretend I am in that park again, sitting unnoticed among the statues. I see the cleaning women pouring out of the subways—hundreds, even thousands of them. It is warm this evening, so maybe they would be walking slowly and laughing as they move toward their places of work. They are truth for me. I want to absorb all that I can learn from them—their values and their commitment and their motivation. And whatever I do in my life, I want to give back to people like them something good.

DELIVERING THE NEWS

I took over Ernie's newspaper route when I was a teenager. He was going off to college, and I rode next to him on my bike for the last few days before he left. Ernie used to take one paper at a time, fold it as he rode and then toss it through the air onto the path or stoop leading to the customer's front door. I noticed that he hardly paused as the papers landed perfectly in the same spot every day, and he never looked back.

His bike had a large metal basket on the handlebars into which he placed a large canvas bag. The bag was white—though many deliveries had faded it to gray—with the lettering "Newark Evening News" in black gothic type on the front. The bag could hold fifty papers on an average day, though I remember that Fridays had especially fat editions and those days were a rough ride. I used to ponder the revelation that the more news there was, the more difficult my life became. (That little shard of wisdom has proved to contain much truth in my life.)

Ernie had a change machine, one of those silvery metal change makers that he wore on a belt. The ice cream man used to have the same kind of thing and such a gadget was long an envy of mine. Without looking, Ernie could count out the exact amount of change and quickly be on his way. On his last day he took me collecting with him and told his customers that he would not be delivering the paper anymore and that—by the way—here was Jeff, who would be taking over the route. I remember people telling him to wait just a minute as they went back into the house and got five or ten dollars for him—a fortune in those days. The customers barely looked at me. I knew I would have to earn my place in their hearts…and pocketbooks.

It has been forty years now since I delivered those papers. The *Newark Evening News* stopped its presses long ago. And I would guess that there are not as many kids delivering papers today as there were back then.

I delivered papers in the 1960s, a time when so much news was heartbreaking. It was a time of war and social upheaval, riots and assassinations. But I was a kid whose interests back then did not move much beyond a new group called the Beatles.

One piece of news was delivered to me, however, that I also absorbed with the unthinking receptivity of a kid. It was the news that there were people like Ernie in the world—people who work hard, are skilled, efficient and dependable, and are kind to others. This is the good news I was given back then, and the memory of it warms me to this day.

I wonder where Ernie is today. He would be a few years older than I am, and I hope life has been kind to him. I'll bet he is still riding without looking back. So much grace has flowed into me from people like Ernie, who never made the news but delivered far more important news than they ever realized.

THE NICKEL VASE

Once, way before I entered the monastery, I went to a writer's conference in Boston. Even then, I guess, I knew that I wanted to communicate with others through the written word rather than by preaching and speaking.

The conference included classes in which the instructor read short stories written by the students. After each story was read, we students would critique it—usually not too insightfully and never very kindly.

One of the participants was a middle-aged woman who sat near me as her story was read. She squirmed and doodled on a pad as her words were absorbed by the class. When the teacher finished the story, the comments began. At first, we were gentle: "The characters are real," "there is a good flow," "the imagery is nice." The woman beamed as if she had finally discovered a group of people who recognized her talent and perceived her inner spirit.

In her story, however, was a five word sentence that read: "The vase cost a nickel." A man raised his hand and harrumphed, "No vase costs only a nickel." The dam was broken, and hands shot up all over the room. There was an outpouring of comments and opinions about the vase—its cost, where it might have been purchased, how it could have been so cheap. The author said nothing but sat doodling with a fury.

Someone said that the price of a nickel threw the rest of the story into a false light. Another claimed to have seen a vase at a flea market in Vermont priced at a mere three cents. Meanwhile, the writer kept making tighter and tighter circles on her notepad.

Finally, she could take it no longer. She stopped her doodling and stood up. Everyone fell silent and stared at her. Her voice cracking with emotion, she swore that the vase had cost her a nickel and that she would never change that detail, even if no one believed her story. Then she started to cry, gathered her things, and stormed out of the room. We never saw her again.

One student commented, "She really got bent out of shape over a measly five cents."

But as I remember the event from behind the cloister walls, I realize that the nickel was never the issue. There were obviously other things going on in the woman's life that our debate triggered. We were all focused on this one detail, and by the time she lost her composure the beauty of her story no longer seemed to matter to anyone but her.

There are a lot of lessons in this little incident. Certainly her fellow students should have been more sensitive and perhaps she should have been less thin-skinned. Maybe the details in an article or story have to be believable, even if we have to manipulate the facts a little to make them so.

But the main thing I took from the incident is the realization that we all cling to apparently insignificant things. When these are threatened or even questioned, it can cause us much pain. There are a lot of "nickel vases" in each of our lives that are important to us alone in ways that no one else can ever understand. Maybe we do not even understand them ourselves. But these vases are easily broken if not handled with care. They are possessions that—taken as a whole—form our personal identity and put us in touch with the inherent goodness we humans share.

So, if someone says that a vase cost a nickel, perhaps we should take that statement at "vase value." (Sorry about the pun, but I couldn't resist.) It may have been worth only small change, but that woman's memory of her vase may have formed the basis for her real wealth.

Do you have eyes, and fail to see?
Do you have ears, and fail to hear?
And do you not remember?

—MARK 8:18

LITTLE STUART

When I was a kid, my family lived on a dead end street ideal for playing all sorts of fantasy games that ended with somebody getting "killed." I particularly remember a little guy named Stuart, who was the king of the dramatic death. Whether pretending to be pierced by an arrow, felled by a bullet, or blasted to smithereens by a ray gun, Stuart would run, turn, twist, circle, clutch, groan, shriek, fall, roll, shake and convulse until he had everyone's attention. Then he would "die" and lie perfectly still for several minutes, until one eye would open and look around furtively to see how his performance had been received.

The small hills near our street were Stuart's favorite place to die, for he could reel around the hilltop, reach pleadingly to the sky, and then finally begin his agonized death descent downwards. At the bottom of the hill he would curl into a ball and lay there letting the tragedy of his demise achieve its full affect.

Stuart's death happened almost every day, often several times a day. (Perhaps he was the forerunner of the kid I hear is always getting killed in the *South Park* cartoon on cable television.) Stuart's personal mortality rate climbed to unheard of peaks on summer days. He liked to be slain, obliterated, murdered, assassinated, wiped out, rubbed out, ambushed, executed, hanged, electrocuted, lethally injected, stabbed, shot, axed, blown up and run over. The only thing he wasn't interested in was a peaceful death.

Stuart also had a fierce temper and would get into one fight after another. I can still see his little arms flailing away. Even then, we all had a sense that Stuart was striking out at something (or someone) much larger and more menacing than his friends or imagined enemies.

Stuart had what we used to call a "club foot." I do not hear the phrase used anymore these days. Perhaps advances in surgery have taken care of this birth defect for most kids, at least in this country. But Stuart lived with that deformity and walked and ran with a slight limp, always favoring his crooked foot.

I wonder even today what caused Stuart to daily invoke the trauma of death and to wrap sorrow around himself like a favorite blanket. The throes of Stuart's many deaths found a place in my heart, and as I have grown older—and especially after I began to practice the Cistercian spirituality—the memory of him remains palpable. Each of us has been born with wounds, some very visible like Stuart's and others hidden even from ourselves. We all share the desire for the world to be a good and safe place, even when we know that it is not always so. Perhaps Stuart's dying fantasies were enacted as a way of playing out the enormous mystery into which we are all born and through which we all run...or limp.

Back in New Jersey, fighter jets used to roar overhead as they approached or departed from Mitchell Field, an Air Force base only minutes away. There was a war going on then, but we had no idea of the intimate connection between what was happening above us and Stuart's dramatic demises. We were only playing; we did not know the deep implications of our daily dramas.

We children could not speak of such things, and we adults mostly do not either. The planes still fly overhead, wars still rage around the world, people are still being executed in our name, the poor still die hungry. And on television any given night, more people pretend to die than Stuart would have ever imagined possible.

No one of the old gang is left on that street now. We all moved to other streets, bringing with us our weaknesses, our limps, our rage, our need for love. I have discovered that the drama that is my own life is born from my own weaknesses. I, too, have had my own episodes of rolling over and playing dead, hoping for a rescue, a dose of sympathy, or at least a drop of attention.

I like to picture Stuart these days, now grown to adulthood, perhaps with his foot miraculously cured, taking a walk on a summer evening with someone he loves. Should they pass two kids fighting on a dead end street, threatening to "kill" each other, I hope Stuart remembers his youthful performances. Perhaps he gently breaks the two kids apart, tells them to shake and make up. Then he takes the arm of the one he loves and they walk slowly, peacefully, quietly toward home, looking up only when a jet roars overhead.

FIRST THINGS FIRST

It was a sunny morning, and light streamed through the tall windows of my first-grade classroom at our Lady of Loretto school in Hempstead, New York.

That morning, like every school day morning, Sister Sheila told the class (of fifty six-year-olds!) to stand and exercise. I'm sure this was her way of both getting rid of some of our nervous energy and waking herself up since she had already been up for four or five hours. (Only since I entered the monastery has the reality of getting up at four or five in the morning occurred to me.)

Sister Sheila stood in the front of the class in full habit and showed us how. "Lift those arms high and stretch, stretch, stretch until you touch the sky," she chirped. So we all lifted our arms and waved them around and tried to touch the sky. "Wiggle your fingers," she called. "Try to tickle the clouds."

David McDonald was my best friend back then, and he sat right in front of me in class. He had a great smile and loved this daily routine. I remember him beaming as he stood and stretched and bowed and twisted each day.

On this particular day, however, David must have forgotten his belt. Or maybe his mom had bought him a new pair of pants that were too large in the waist. In any case, as he tried to touch the sky and tickle the clouds, suddenly his pants fell down straight to his ankles. With something approaching the speed of light, he bent down, grabbed his pants, pulled them up, held them with one hand, and resumed stretching with the other. As

I sit here and think about it, I am laughing out loud. It may have been the single funniest thing I have ever witnessed. It was like watching a movie that has been speeded up to the nth degree.

But still his moves were not fast enough. The kids behind us saw what happened, and squeals and laughter filled the room. First-grade girls put their hands to their mouths in utter 1950s Catholic shock. First-grade boys roared in 1950s Catholic delight. David blushed. I froze. Sister Sheila, who had missed the entire thing, shrieked "Siiiiilennncccccce!" (I'm pretty sure that's how the word she yelled is spelled.)

Order was immediately restored, but exercise was over for the day. We all sat down and pulled out our Dick and Jane readers and got back to work—except for an occasional titter from a girl or guffaw from a boy. David remained mortified the rest of the day, but he eventually milked the incident for all the laughs he could get. I'll bet he tells the story to his grandkids.

What I remember about that day (in order of importance) are: first, that the funniest things in life are neither planned nor spoken; second, how powerful a single word said with authority and conviction can be; third, how fast we humans can move when caught with our pants down; and fourth, if there is a choice between touching the heavens and covering our butts, we instinctively will lunge for the latter.

GOOD

She was a waitress in a Shanghai restaurant, and "good" was the only English word she knew. It was a year after the Tianneman Square uprising, when people all over the world watched a horrible confrontation that ended in the slaughter of innocent people by the Chinese government.

I was in China on a tour, and the hesitancy of the Chinese people was obvious. They were afraid to be seen even talking with any foreigner, especially an American. Chinese military men and women seemed to be everywhere, watching every move of tourist and native alike. Our Chinese guides, bona fide members of the Communist party, never once mentioned or even alluded to the Tianneman tragedy. Virtually everyone acted as if it had never happened.

The particular restaurant where the waitress worked was small but busy. She was eager to please but very nervous. She smiled shyly as she approached our table, and our guide spoke with her in Chinese. Then he smiled at us and said, "Just point to what you want from the menu, and she will get it for you." We looked at the menu and saw that there were drawings of ducks, pigs, fish, shrimp, vegetables, and other foods. So we pointed out what we wanted.

"Good," she said as the first person in our party ordered. "Good," she said again at the second order, then the next, and after each subsequent one. "Good, good, good," she repeated.

I asked our guide if the woman knew any more English, and he fired off something in Chinese to her. The waitress shook her head. "She only knows 'good' and what 'good' means," our guide replied, missing the irony completely. "Good," I responded.

The food was brought and the waitress hovered within ear-shot (and finger-pointing shot) lest we want for anything. But we all smiled and ate and drank, nodding to her often and saying "good" several times each. She beamed each time we did so, with a blend of genuine pleasure and relief. "Good," she said, when we finally finished, paid our bill, and got up to leave.

There are many things I remember about my trip to China. I was astounded by the vastness of its countryside, the breadth of its history, the throngs of people we saw, the size of its cities, the beauty of its art and architecture. I also remember the fear that hung in the air and the sense that the entire society was being run by a tiny fraction of its huge population.

But the main thing I remember was summed up by that one waitress. To her, everything was "good," and that is a real theological statement—one that fits Cistercian spirituality to a T. It is goodness that humanizes and heals us all, goodness that bridges cultures and politics and menus of any language.

It was Chairman Mao himself who said that one match can ignite a prairie. I believe that some day that waitress's one word, "good," will change the entire world in ways that Mao and his successors never thought possible.

DELIVERING THE GOODS

During my summers while in the seminary, one of the jobs I had was delivering beer for Anheuser-Busch. It was not steady work but rather what the union guys called "shape-up." Every morning, fifty or so men (plus one seminarian) would gather in a shed just inside the main gate of the Budweiser brewery located on Route 9, just across from Newark International Airport. I was at the low end of the totem pole, but every once in a while I got a job for the day.

The pay was great, I knew my way around the north Jersey area, and I felt like a big shot driving a truck full of beer. One day though, I had trouble finding a street in what the locals call the Down Neck section of Newark. I zigzagged my way up and down a bunch of parallel streets named after American presidents, going under several viaducts that carried commuter train tracks. I carefully noted the signs on each bridge indicating its height to make sure that there was enough room for the truck to pass.

I cannot remember the name of the street where it happened—Garfield? Polk? Bush? Gore?—but whatever street it was must have been recently repaved. For, sure enough, the height was slightly less than the sign indicated, which I discovered the minute the bottom of the bridge tore off the top of the truck.

There's nothing like hitting a bridge to bring a big truck to a dead stop. Another guy was riding with me, and both our heads hit the windshield. We sat there in a mild state of shock, and he turned to me and stated the obvious: "You hit the bridge." With an equal amount of insight, I answered, "I know." It was one of the few statements in my life that I have been absolutely sure of.

A crowd quickly gathered. This was apparently not a first-time experience for them. We climbed out of the truck and looked at the roof, now crumpled like an accordion. Many things went through my mind: the loss of my summer job, having to pay damages, driving through Newark with the truck top sheared off, returning to the brewery and having everyone laugh at me.

Some kid starting letting the air out of the tires, and eventually I was able to ease the truck away from the bridge. I yelled thanks to the kid and he asked for a free case of beer. I told him no, so he gave me the finger and ran off. The crowd began to disperse.

"Better call in," my partner said. So I found a nearby phone and called the dispatcher. He was pretty dispassionate about the whole thing.

"Are you okay?" he asked.

"Yeah," I answered.

"Is your partner okay?"

"Yeah."

"Can you drive the truck?"

"Yeah."

"Was much of the beer ruined?

"Yeah, I mean, no," I answered, not really knowing the true situation. I didn't see anything dripping from the truck, however.

"Well, a little sunshine won't hurt the beer, and those

trucks aren't ours anyway," the dispatcher explained. "We rent them, and they'll just give us another one. So just get the beer delivered and fill out a form when you get back."

Then he hung up. I felt both relief and dismay. Relief that I wasn't about to be fired and apparently didn't have to pay for the damage. Dismay because I guess I expected some form of expression of personal concern, but all that seemed to matter was getting the beer delivered.

In retrospect, I don't know what I wanted from the dispatcher. He wasn't about to jump in a car and come comfort me, and I had told him that my partner and I were all right and that the beer was fine. So why shouldn't we deliver the goods?

And so it was that my partner and I drove the rest of the route with people gawking at the beer truck with no top. When we returned at the end of the day, there were predictable stares and guffaws from a few of our colleagues, but most of them really couldn't have cared less what happened, and probably more than a couple of them had done the same thing once or twice in their careers.

As I look back on my life and all the different routes I have taken, I realize the many mistakes I have made—from miscalculation, from misreading the signs, from worrying too much about what other people thought of me. But there has always been some version of the kid who let the air out of the tires to get me back on the road. (Maybe I should have given him at least one beer.)

The main thing I learned from this episode, however, is not to feel sorry for myself. There are still times when the top of my world seems to be ripped off, but if I look closely I can see that "the goods" are still intact and that a little sunshine won't hurt them. My job is to get back in the truck and deliver them.

SO BIG

I am one of six children in my family, and I can remember playing "so big" with my younger sister and brothers when they were babies. You remember the game: You ask a baby how big someone is, and then you hold his or her arms out as wide as you can and say "so big."

"How big is baby?" you ask.

"So big," baby answers.

"How big is Father James?"

"So big."

The game is fun, endless, and works all the time. Babies seem to have a natural and ecstatic response to it. I still play it with every baby I come in contact with. I think babies get the idea that "so big" is as big as things get, that the span of their little arms is the essence of "bigness," that identifying how big things are is a sure way to please the funny adults and older children surrounding them. In their developing minds, the equation goes like this: "so big" = right answer = pleasing the other = laughter, kisses, hugs = let's do it again.

For many of us, however, the definition of bigness changes as we get older. Big salaries, big cars and homes, big stock portfolios, big jobs, big deals, and big egos become the measure of how right things are in our lives. But there is another way to play this game, and that is to ask, "How big is the heart of God?" The answer, of course, is "so big."

I looked about me this morning at our monastery church and the people in it. The monks were there, as well as folks from the area and our overnight visitors. The walls towered above us, light poured through the stained glass windows, the smell of incense lingered in the air. We were part of a religious tradition that is thousands of years old. It was a living fresco of the human search for God.

But all we know is that we really know very little about God. Maybe we have exhausted the meaning of the very words we use to describe the divine reality, or maybe they never were adequate. Perhaps images for the Godhead no longer have the power and clarity they had in former times. Is God someone we think we shall someday "find" or "comprehend" or "measure" with our seeking? Or is divinity so overwhelmingly that we simply cannot get our minds and our souls around it?

I think the babies have it right with their game. God's existence and love is far beyond our ability to comprehend. Yet we can continue to stretch our own hearts to the point of breaking in our search, knowing that we will receive nothing but goodness and hugs in return. "So big" is a game we can play over and over and over again without ever tiring of it.

THE LADY WHO LOVED PAPERBACKS

Before I moved to the monastery, I used to sit in my rectory back in Newark and try to write. There was one woman who used to sit in an old beach chair on the sidewalk in front of her apartment building, and I could see her from my office window almost every day in the warmer seasons. I guessed her to be in her late seventies, and I figured she lived on her social security checks and not much else. On hot days, she wore a baseball cap, and on breezy days she had a pretty scarf that kept her wispy hair in place. She always wore a cotton print dress in a lovely shade of one color or another.

What I remember about her is that she loved to read and always had a paperback book with her. Sitting at my computer and stuck on a sentence, I would often gaze out my window and my eyes would invariably come to rest on her. There was something simple and beautiful about the way she read. Every so often she would gently close the book and, with her finger keeping her place, she would raise her head and with a dream-like smile take in her surroundings. It was as if she had been deeply refreshed from her excursion into the world offered by her book and was bringing the life she had found there onto the street we shared.

I once saw her in a nearby used bookstore that I frequented. I didn't have the guts to introduce myself, but I peeked at the selection of books she purchased. There were novels by Faulkner, Cather, Welty, Hemingway. I heard her ask the cashier whether a title by the Japanese author Shusaku Endo was ever available. (I made a mental note of the name and later bought several books by that magical writer.)

I wondered what the woman did with the books after she read them. Did she trade them in for other novels? Did she give them away to friends? Was her apartment filled with treasures? Later, I thought of her heart as a treasure house and how she shared her delight in reading with others by the simple fact of reading on the street. When she raised her head from a book that had transformed her, she transformed her own world with her pleasure.

What I learned from the woman who loved paperbacks is that the mystery of being is flowing through us and around us, both in the imaginary world of literature and in the real world we inhabit. We are in that river and moving with it. She was my river pilot, teaching me the connection between the written word and lived experience.

She and I never exchanged a word, but I think of her every time I write. Wondrous, isn't it, that she gave me something so beautiful, something that I now try to pass on to others.

I hope, wherever she is today, that her chair is comfortable and the breezes gentle and that she has something good to read. If I could, I would send her my book, with the hope that she might look up from it once or twice and smile.

CREAKS

When I was a kid, I shared a room with my twin brother, Jimmy, on the third floor of one of those big old houses found all over the Northeast. I remember specifically the sound of the heat hissing and banging as it made its way on a winter morning through the basement pipes and upward through the house and finally into the large iron radiator that stood against the wall of our room. Dad used to place water pans behind the radiator to replace the moisture that the heat fried away. Without that water, the air in our room became as dry and arid as any desert's.

That house had a music of its own. Each different door made a unique sound as it opened and closed. The slapping sound of feet on the red linoleum floor in the hall and kitchen softened as someone entered the adjacent carpeted rooms. I can summon the sound of newspaper pages being folded as Dad read them one by one or of change jangling in his pocket when he got up from the couch. The sound of his Zippo lighter flipping open was unmistakable, as was the sound of the switch when he turned on his reading lamp.

In college, there were many nights when I came home much later than I should have. As I neared the house, I made preparations for as quiet an entry as possible. I took the coins from my pocket and left them on the front seat of the car. I removed the one key I needed for the front door from the key ring, inserted it just right into the lock, and turned it ever so slowly to mute the tell-tale click. Rusty, our dog, would be lying on the rug in the front hall. He would sleepily raise his head, yawn, wag his tail, and get up to investigate. I would pat him on the head, put my finger to my lips, and back down he'd go.

Then I'd start to climb the stairs to the third floor. It took some time—and a few time getting caught—but eventually I got to know every crack and weak spot on those polished wooden stairs. It got so I knew exactly where to step and not to step, which slight shifts left or right avoided the tell-tale creaks and allowed a silent ascent to my bedroom. The key was getting past Mom and Dad's bedroom on the second floor. If I could hear snoring from both of them (both of them different sounds, of course), I knew I had it made. My grandmother's room was right near theirs, but I never worried about her because she never squealed. The next morning, she would just give me a knowing look and a wry smile.

It's funny how I can still hear specific sounds even today. I lay awake at the monastery, listening to the creaks and moans of the old buildings, hearing the monks pacing up and down in the hallways, catching the cry of a night owl or the buzzing of an insect, and remember that old house of my childhood. It was a place full of the sound of grace.

We get through life by way of our senses. In fact, they are the only way that we can ever come to know God. Through them we touch, hear, smell, taste, and see the world around us, the world we have been given as pure gift. Through them we absorb meaning, love, wonder and joy.

I often wonder if paradise will be a place in which our senses will somehow operate. I hope so. I hope that we will continue to absorb all that is holy and beautiful, slowly and with care, through senses—even if they are different from the five we are used to. The goodness of this life comes to us through our senses, I hope the same is true of the next.

When I die, I'd like to be able to pull out a key to heaven, turn it softly in the lock of the pearly gates, and sneak up the stairs to my loved ones.

BEATTIE

Her name was Beattie, short for Beatrice, which means "beautiful," and she was. Beattie was in her seventies and was the housekeeper in the rectory I lived in. She had lost her husband many years before and raised their only son to adulthood. She and I got along very well.

Beattie's life was one of many hardships, but she was a real survivor (not like those phony "survivors" I heard about on the television series). She knew how to beautify what little she had. With a nice dress and a new hairdo and a splash of cologne, she was always able to fashion herself with dignity, and no small part of her beauty was the ease with which she shared it with everyone.

Beattie used to go through rough times and needed to talk them out. For some reason she chose me. I would be sitting at the dining room table and could sense that it was a day she needed to vent. She would come into the house, looking a bit down, unload her bag of groceries on the table, and make coffee. Then she would pour two cups and bring them in, sit down across from me, and ask, "Are you busy?" Without awaiting a reply, she would look out the window as if summoning her thoughts from somewhere far away. Then she would turn to me and begin. Usually she would talk non-stop for fifteen or twenty minutes, going over what was by then mostly familiar terrain: losing her husband early, being ignored by her friends, being verbally abused by someone at the grocery store, the many failures of her legendary car.

I would listen and nod, occasionally looking out the window to see how many more words were gathered on the horizon. Then I would glance back at Beattie, who was by then near tears, and just smile, hoping something she might see in me or something I might say would help. All our "conversations" ever seemed to do was confirm her firmly held conviction that things never change one little bit.

Finally, though, she would finish, wipe her eyes, blow her nose, and say, "Thank you, Father. You're a nice boy." The amazing thing was that she then appeared to be fine, even aglow, for much of the rest of the day and into the next.

Beattie passed away a few years ago. I do not think that any of her problems were every really solved. They just piled up until they got too high, then she found someone on whom to unload them, and then they lost their claim on her spirit.

I learned from Beattie that few things in life ever really change. Yet the talking out of our hurts to someone who will listen transforms them into something more tolerable. It's like the burdens of living become lighter just by sharing them.

Even though I've now taken the vow of silence, there are still times when I find a friend, pour him or her a proverbial cup of coffee, and say, "Are you busy?" And, bless Beattie's heart, it always seems to help. Words do many things, and at least one of those things is magical: Words build living bridges across which we humans meet and heal one another.

THE CONEY ISLAND PUB

In the west of Ireland, near Bushtown in Glenamaddy, is a large field, and in the middle of that field is the Coney Island Pub. I went there many years ago, and I learned something about myself.

I was with another Irish-American friend (the name Behrens is German, although my mother's a Sullivan) who had some cousins he had never met in Ireland, and one evening we drove through many small towns to get to the pub to meet them. Finally, we turned onto the last dirt road that was on the pencil-drawn map we had been given. We couldn't see anything at first except the field, but as we drove a little further we came across a sign that had an arrow and the words "To the C. I. Pub: Approach with Care."

So we turned onto the field itself, and sure enough we discovered that there was something that passed for a road beneath the wheels of the car, although it was really only where the grass had been matted down by cars that had passed before us. We soon came upon an odd-looking building that we couldn't see from the road. It was built like a bunker—close to the ground and seemingly impenetrable. There was one door and a few windows, all of them open and streaming light from the inside. Several cars—which we had also not seen—were parked outside. The whole thing reminded me of the vanishing land in the musical *Brigadoon*.

As we got out of our car, we heard laughter and singing coming from the pub. It was a delightful sound, almost magical in quality. Little did I know that the magic was only about to begin. All around us the Irish sky was turning a rich red with the setting of the sun. The lush greens and browns of the field were speckled with gold as the sun's rays played off the moisture from an afternoon shower that clung to every leaf, weed, and blade of grass. If there were ever a night and a place that could entice me to believe in the legendary Irish myths, it would be that night around the Coney Island Pub.

We walked through the door and found a room filled with people. They all looked up. A few waved or smiled at us, and some raised their mugs of beer in welcome. A haze of cigarette smoke drifted in the air, one long wisp slowly drifting beneath the single large light fixture on the ceiling. The room was hot, but not uncomfortably so, and my companion and I took an empty table.

There didn't seem to be any kind of waiter or even a traditional bar, but we soon spotted a hole in the wall through which an arm would periodically emerge with a bottle of beer that one of the customers would grab. A young man came over to us and said, "You must be the Americans. Paddy is waiting to welcome you in the back room." He nodded in the direction of the hole in the wall. There, behind a table of especially boisterous men, we spotted a door that was slightly ajar. We peeked in and saw the proprietor with three other men, who turned out to be my friend's distant cousins, sitting around a small table. Smiles lit all their faces as we tentatively entered the back room, and they made room for the two of us at the crowded table. Everyone introduced themselves around, and Paddy brought out beers for everyone. He beamed at the opportunity to host a first meeting of blood relatives in his establishment.

I was the odd man out, but I felt at home with these men, who like the apostle Nathaniel were "without guile." It occurred to me as I sat there that I had not been treated like a stranger once while in Ireland—a land in which I knew absolutely no one before I arrived. It seems that the Irish have a natural instinct for healing human estrangement. Ireland is a place of openness: open faces and smiles, open doors and windows, open souls to God's grace (which I think they would define as whatever God brings).

My friend and I chatted for a while about our trip, our respective homes and families, what we each knew about our Irish ancestry (which wasn't much). The men knew that we were both priests, and I had the feeling that this knowledge put a slight restraint on where the conversation might have gone, but I considered this to be a sign of respect for the Church and their religious heritage.

"Well," said Paddy (and that was his real name, I wouldn't make that up), "the fun is about to begin. Come with me." We followed him and the others into the larger room. Everyone was now sitting in a circle three to five people deep. There was a lone, straight-backed chair in the center of the circle, directly beneath the one light fixture, still swirling with smoke. Honest to God, it looked like something out of an old Humphrey Bogart movie.

Seats of honor had been reserved for us, and soon a young woman stood up and walked slowly to the chair in the center. She stopped right in front of the chair, looked around at the group with a gaze that showed not a bit of fear or self-consciousness, fixed a wisp of her hair with her hand, smiled, and then started to sing. Her voice was the closest I have ever heard to that of an angel. She sang a sad Irish song about a boy who went away and never returned. She easily convinced me that she was singing with a heart broken by the loss of her own true love. When she finished, applause and cheers filled the room, and a feeling of love did too. She bowed and took her seat again.

A young man got up from his seat and went to the center chair. He too looked around and smiled with confidence. He sang a song about a young woman's beauty—her hair, her eyes, her lips and how she used them. He finished and bowed to the same applause and cheering as the woman had received.

Thus it went as the night went on. Different people did different things. Some sang, some told stories, others told jokes. One man got up and spoke very matter-of-factly about a miracle he had experienced: The Blessed Mother had spoken to him in a dream. A hush fell over the room as he spoke, and after he finished the applause was different—more reverential than anything else, and certainly without a hint of doubt or derision.

Near the end of the evening, Paddy leaned over and asked me if I had a song or a story to share. I sheepishly declined. He told me that some day I would be ready to share what and who I am. He winked as he said it. It was a "you wait and see" kind of wink.

And that's what I learned that night. After "waiting and seeing" for many years, I realize that Paddy was right. How I wish I had been free enough, confident enough, centered enough, to get up and share a piece of myself with those wonderful people at the Coney Island Pub. They would not have judged me. They would have accepted me as one of them, just as they accepted everyone else that night. It is the patrons of Paddy's pub who have given me the permission and the courage to write, to put out who and what I am before others, to trust that my words will be accepted for what they are—no more and no less.

As my friend and I drove out of the pub and onto the road, there was another sign: "Leave with Gratitude and Care." I certainly did.

CONCLUSION

I was in bed last evening waiting for sleep to come. There was a full moon, and its light poured into my room like a soft silver glow. I lay there thinking about the day's activities, not focusing on anything particular.

Then the past came flooding into my mind, as it does many nights here in Conyers. The memories of all the grace I have experienced in my life started to warm me, and I began to wonder if the memories themselves are a form of prayer.

I thought back to the night my father was dying and my mother and brothers and sisters and I were all there in the hospital room. I remember feeling a similar warmth. The day before, Dad had asked me how he would know how to find—"on the other side"—my twin brother Jimmy, who had died in a car accident when we were both teenagers. I said that Jimmy would come and find him.

I remember Dad crying when he asked me to help him pick out what Jimmy should wear when he was buried. But I remember other things, too, like the time Jimmy and I were in early high school and Dad brought us to New York to buy our first suits. Then he took us to his office on Fifth Avenue and introduced us to the people with whom he worked. I remember how proud he was of us and how proud we were of him.

Jimmy died long ago, but I still dream about him often. I have heard that means there is some sort of unfinished business between us, and I'm sure that is true. Maybe that is partly why I took his name when I entered the monastery.

After I finally fell asleep last night, I dreamed that Jimmy and I went to Europe. I didn't have a valid passport, but Jimmy smiled and said not to worry. It all seemed so natural. He is always young when I dream of him, nor do I realize in my dreams that he is dead. I want to say to him, "Jimmy, my story is your story. My memories are your memories."

ACKNOWLEDGMENTS

"If you want to play outside then first spend time inside the house and write those thank-you notes," said my mom many times, many years ago. And so I wrote and then I played. But as the years passed I came to enjoy the writing as much as the playing. So I thank Mom for making me write first and play later. Now, here in the "later," I also thank:

- My editor, Greg Pierce, and everyone at ACTA Publications, and the staffs at the *National Catholic Reporter*, *Living Faith*, *St. Anthony Messenger*, *The Liguorian*, *Notre Dame Magazine*, *Spirit and Life*, and other publications that have helped me shape and share my words.

- Those whose love and encouragement moved me to think something good was at play in my writing: Mary Dwyer (my godmother); Joan Chittister, OSB; Dolores Leckey; Dick Liddy; Archbishop Peter Leo Gerety; Bernard Johnson, OCSO; Andre Dubus; Walker Percy; John Monczunski; Anne Lamott; Karen Leibnitz; as well as John Arnold; Michael Farrell; Teresa Malcolm; Tom Fox; John Allen; Francis Michael Stiteler, OCSO; Patrick Hart, OCSO; Damian Turk, OCSO; Patrick Samway, SJ; Mark Neilsen; Ward Moore; Frank Goss; Joe and Anita Puglisis; Susan McBride; Valerie O'Reilly; Pat Ryan; Peggy and Walt Bomhoff; Fredrick Gartner; and all my brother monks here at Conyers.

- Those whose lives generously offer the beauty that is grace to written words: PeeWee McCollum, J.P. McIsaac, Beatrice Palperio, Anna Sullivan, Jean and Carl Kalemba, Steve and Claire Filipow, Emmanuel Capozzelli, Geralyn Barnett, Steve and Anne Barron.

There are more. You know who you are. I thank you, too.

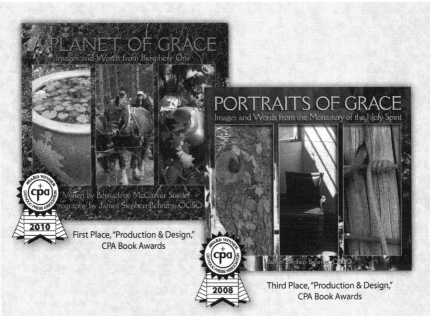